CW01646219

IMPORTANT: PLEASE READ

Information provided in this Guide is for educational purposes. It is not intended to replace the advice or instruction of a health care professional, or to substitute for medical care. Contact a health care professional if you have any questions regarding your care.

Second edition, June 2023

DEDICATION

To all the people living with dementia
and
To all their care partners

You inspire us to be more, be better, be stronger

"One of the basic rules of the universe is that nothing is perfect. Perfection simply doesn't exist...

Without imperfection, neither you nor I would exist."

— Stephen Hawking

Foreword

This is a Guide about dementia. **And it's been written especially for you**, those living with a dementia diagnosis and their care partners. The term Major Neurocognitive Disorder is increasingly used in some health care systems, but we made a decision to use the more familiar term dementia throughout this text.

As doctors and consultants in the field, we've come to realize that a shift in focus is needed to communicate about dementia in an accessible and thoughtful way, one that provides education and guidelines for best care practices. It is one of the primary objectives of the McGill Dementia Education Program.

A genuine partnership must be established between:

1. People living with dementia
2. Care partners
3. Health care professionals

A dementia diagnosis challenges everyone. The only way to successfully navigate it all is to form a united front that empowers us to make positive, lasting changes now and for the future.

Three things need to happen:

1. Prioritize the necessity for acceptance, compassion and kindness.
2. Amplify the call for public information, prevention and support.
3. Make research and education an ongoing imperative.

Allies today, allies tomorrow, allies forever.

A dementia diagnosis is an initiation into a baffling world. This Guide aims to help with that transition through a comprehensive approach as well as provide counsel on strategies to manage it successfully.

This Guide is divided into two sections:

1. Support and education for the person living with dementia
2. Support and education for care partners

We hope that within these pages, you'll find that solid foundation to build on when dealing with a dementia diagnosis - and cultivate everyday practices to contribute to a **quality of life that translates to a life well lived**.

We would like to thank the Grace Dart Foundation for their vision and support. Their generous contribution has funded the creation, production and translation of this valuable educational resource, *Dementia, Your Companion Guide*, and enabled us to make it freely available in both print and online formats on our website at www.mcgill.ca/dementia, and through clinicians in the McGill- affiliated network. To learn more about the Grace Dart Foundation, please visit their website at www.fondationgracedart.com.

The Dementia Education Program would like to extend their gratitude to everyone who assisted with the creation of this Guide. In particular, we would like to thank Ms. Mona Atallah, Mr. Matt Evans, Ms. Leila Zahabi, Ms. Diane Weidner and Ms. Joanne Lavallée, respectively for their valuable roles in writing, illustrating, coordinating, proofreading and translating this Guide. We would also like to thank Prof. Tamara Carver, Ms. Zeina Salameh, and Ms. Maria Vincelli, along with McGill University's Steinberg Centre for Simulation and Interactive Learning and the Office of Education Technology and E-learning Collaboration for Health, for their guidance and support.

Dr José A. Morais
Professeur, Faculté de médecine et des sciences de la santé, Université McGill
Directeur, Division de gériatrie, Centre universitaire de santé McGill et Hôpital général juif
Responsable académique, Programme de formation sur les troubles neurocognitifs de l'Université McGill

Dr Serge Gauthier
Professeur émérite en neurologie et psychiatrie, Université McGill
Co-responsable académique, Programme de formation sur les troubles neurocognitifs de l'Université McGill

Mme Claire Webster
Conseillère certifiée en soins des troubles neurocognitifs
Fondatrice, Passage Aidant
Fondatrice et ambassadrice, Programme de formation sur les troubles neurocognitifs de l'Université McGill

Table of Contents

Section I: The person living with dementia

Section II: Care Partners

Section I: The Person Living with Dementia

Understanding Dementia

The "prescription of care" contained in these pages consists of education, tools and recommendations to help you understand and manage what is ahead.

There is one thing you should unequivocally know right now. **This diagnosis does not define ALL of you.** You can and will continue to enjoy a fulfilling life. And family and friends will continue to enjoy spending time with you.

The journey starts and this Guide will accompany you every step of the way.

This first part is all about you - the person who has been diagnosed.

There is much to learn about dementia and we will steer you through it all with dignity, respect and empathy. **Our goal is to take good care of you.**

It begins.

So, something happened.

Did you misplace your keys one too many times?

Did you look into your son's face and it took a few seconds to remember his name?

Maybe you forgot your way home from the store?

And is that why you're now sitting in your doctor's office waiting for results?

Could it be dementia, you wonder?

Why Me?

Any person receiving a life-altering diagnosis is bound to ask themselves this question. You most certainly have.

Dementia, like many other illnesses, is constantly evolving as scientists conduct complex research and studies to answer this very simple question.

Here's what we know now

Dementia is not one disease

Rather, **it is a group of symptoms** that happen because of a disease. These symptoms manifest through cognitive impairments and decline. Basically, dementia accelerates the natural changes that an aging or injured brain undergoes.

Simply put, **cognition is the process of thinking**. It's how your brain brings all your knowledge, perceptions, decision-making skills, judgement, reasoning, imagery, language and memory together – and how that impacts your actions and behaviour. That may sound like a lot, but this process is constantly happening in the background. As soon as you wake up in the morning, it starts.

For instance, within a couple of minutes, you may have already made many decisions and plans to organize your day such as:

- Chosen to have tea instead of coffee;
- Opted for a bath instead of a shower;
- Decided on going to the bookstore first and then the dry cleaners because it was closer;
- Looked out the window and realized it was colder than predicted. Put away your blue sweater and set aside your coat instead;

- Added four more people to your anniversary party guest list and left a message for your son to drop off more chairs;
- Reminded yourself to call your bank at 10 a.m. about your RRSP account.

When this process is **impaired**, these types of decisions and choices may be harder or more time-consuming to accomplish. You may have trouble remembering facts or concentrating on what you're doing. Your ability to juggle several details at once may lessen. Dementia occurs when this impairment progresses to the point that it interferes with your everyday life and impacts your actions and behaviour in an adverse way.

Dementia is the loss or destruction of nerve cells and their connection to the brain. When that connection is skewed or lost, **your thinking, behaviour and feelings become affected**. You may have started to experience this very thing.

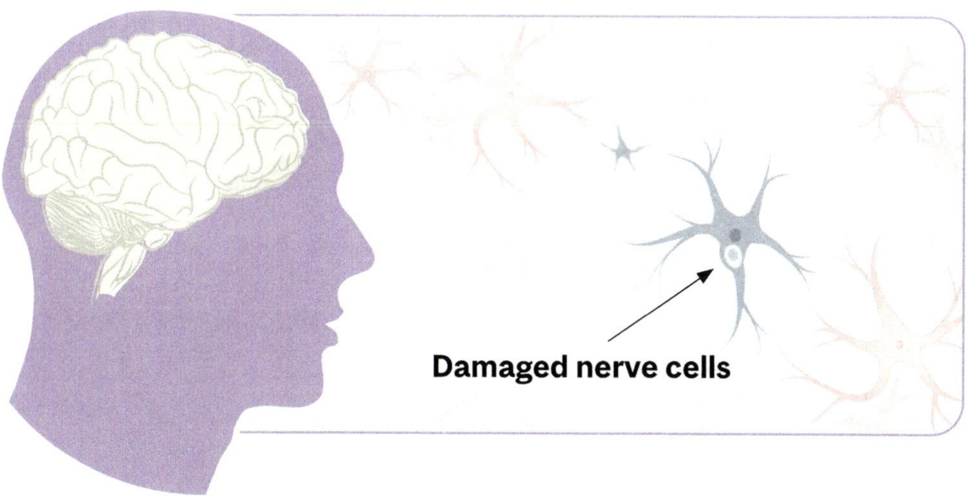

Think of it like your favorite necklace. You've had it around your neck for years and years. But over long-time wear, the links may stretch and the metal becomes weak. The connection is dulled or lost.

Age is the leading contributing factor to developing dementia

Have you wondered why we hear about it more now than ever before? We are living longer, and not by just a few years, but by many. It's not unusual these days to hear of someone celebrating their 100th birthday.

After World War II, advances in hygiene (cleaner drinking water, better sanitation measures) and nutrition (more variety and availability of healthier foods) were coupled with the advent of antibiotics. This greatly extended our life expectancy, and with it, instances of dementia increased.

That's why 30% of people over 85 have some form of dementia.

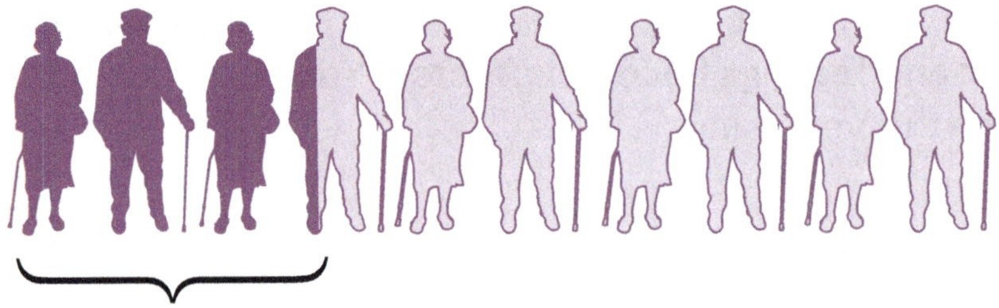

Dementia is progressive

albeit at different rates. Symptoms will increase over time. This applies to both your physical and mental states. How you approach your daily activities and relationships with others will inevitably change. But there are things you can do about that, and you will learn about them in this Guide.

Understanding your illness is a valuable tool. It arms you with information to help you make the necessary choices for how you live today and in the future.

There's much to think about in the pages to come - a great deal to process as you take in this diagnosis and its impact on you. Take your time. Take a breath. When you're ready, we'll start together.

In this first section intended for you, the person living with dementia, we'll go over some new terms you may encounter during your diagnosis as well as the different causes, stages and symptoms of dementia and associated conditions. Topics such as your safety, driving, social life, self-care and strategies for your overall well-being will also be addressed.

Thinking about dementia necessarily means rethinking so many aspects of your life - independence, work, family, finances. **Everything that shapes your world, really.**

We'll provide you with ideas and recommendations to help navigate these ongoing adjustments.

When it's time to start building your support network, let this Guide be part of that. Like we said, we want to take good care of you.

> "A lack of education about dementia will have a significant impact on the quality of care as well as the safety of the individuals and their care partners."

— Claire Webster
Founder & Ambassador, McGill University
Dementia Education Program

An important distinction

Syndrome – We've already stated that dementia is a group of related symptoms that come about because of a disease. Not every person will exhibit the exact same set of symptoms leading to their diagnosis and even throughout their illness. And that ambiguity, **the absence of a clear cause and effect**, is why it is called a syndrome. Let's put that into a relatable context.

"All roads lead to Rome" or at least somewhere that matters to you. It's your granddaughter's birthday. At exactly 2:15 p.m., you're driving northbound on the highway, your niece is sitting on a bus from the south shore and your best friend just hailed a downtown cab - all of you headed to join the celebration. This network of roads will get all of you to your same destination.

And that is where you are right now - having navigated a series of interwoven symptoms like memory loss, confusion and personality changes that at some point merge together, it has led you, and people like you, to the same place - dementia syndrome.

Dementia is an equal opportunity syndrome that can happen to anyone. It does not discriminate based on gender, economic status, sexual preference, geography or ethnicity. Yes, dementia does affect older people more, but younger people are not entirely immune.

Disease – Few of us have escaped the clutches of some disease or another in our lifetime, so the word will not be as foreign sounding to you.

You may have been feeling under the weather or had some pain that has led you to your doctor's clinic. After visual observation, discussion and a physical examination, he or she will complete the visit by ordering a series of tests to assess and measure your symptoms. This could include blood tests, urine samples or scans.

Results in hand, they can determine that you have a **disease, namely a health condition that has a known cause**. What makes these results all the more significant is that they also rule out other potential medical issues. And with a disease, the symptoms, progressions and ensuing treatments have usually already been predetermined. This could include anything from prescribing medication like antibiotics, physical therapy, referrals to specialists and even surgery.

Here's where it gets interesting. Different diseases can trigger dementia, the most common being Alzheimer's disease, accounting for 60-80% of the cases in older adults. In the next two chapters, we'll examine the different stages of dementia, and then embark upon an exploration of Alzheimer's disease as well as the other conditions and diseases that can lead to a dementia diagnosis.

The Language of Dementia

Your doctors and care partners will play key roles throughout the course of your illness. But no one, especially at the beginning, will be more instrumental in your care development than **YOU**.

A slew of unfamiliar terms and concepts will be aimed your way. Actively engaging in mastering all things dementia as well as the required steps needed for your own well-being, both emotional and physical, should not be devalued by you or anyone else. Find your voice and let yourself be heard. Often.

Make a list of the questions you want to ask your doctor on your next visit. Take a family member or friend with you to take notes, help clarify information and provide emotional support.

Ask that the information be explained to you slowly and with diagrams, if necessary.

– Société Alzheimer du Canada

After diagnosis, the discussion should naturally lead to the different aspects of the illness - including where you are in the dementia spectrum. This refers to how your symptoms manifest, their level of severity, what that means and what to expect.

Your doctor will then recommend appropriate treatment and helpful information to minimize the effects of your symptoms.

Normal aging process

As you get older, every part of you slows down. It is one of those things that makes us all alike. Whether it be diminished brain function or physical abilities like flexibility and endurance, there's no denying that joints stiffen, muscles weaken and that we tire more easily.

Everything takes a little bit longer. That's also why your responses and reactions are more considered. Like climbing those stairs, your thought processes require additional effort and recall. For example, you may:

- Occasionally have difficulty finding a specific word. You may use a few descriptors to jog your memory when having a conversation;
- Need a little more time to process information;
- Be slower to think and do things;
- Be hesitant from time to time;

- Be a little impulsive at times;
- Recognize the acquaintance in front of you but have a hard time recalling their name;
- Be unable to remember details of a conversation or event that took place a year ago;
- Forget things and events every now and again;
- Be worried about your memory, though your friends and relatives are not concerned.

None of these things noticeably disrupt your daily life. Ascertaining that these changes are not dementia, or accompany a dementia diagnosis, can only be determined by your doctor.

Stages

There are three distinct stages of dementia and your health care professional will determine which one you are in based on the progression of your symptoms. Though dementia is different for every person, these stages provide insight on some universal changes brought on by dementia.

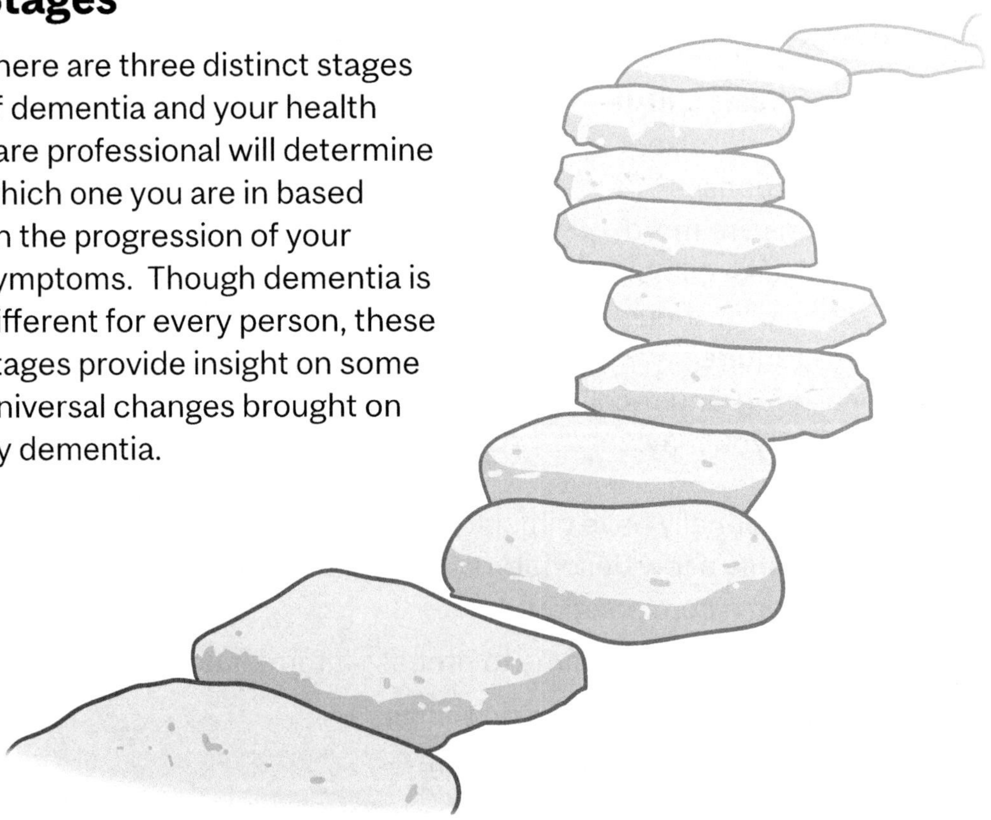

The stages are **guidelines for health care professionals** - doctors, nurses and researchers - to be unified in their understanding, approach and treatment of dementia, be it on a local or global level. Collaboration is key to making needed advancements.

By the same token, these **guidelines allow you** to get a clear handle on your diagnosis, validate what you have already gone through and inform you on what to expect.

Each stage has its own set of adjustments and challenges. As an individual, the length of time you spend in each stage, the collection of symptoms you have, and the advancement from one stage to another will most certainly vary. Stages can last months or years.

Now that you know the overall framework of why there are stages, we're going to delve deeper and differentiate each one.

Stages of Dementia Defined

Early Stage (Mild)

You or someone in your inner circle may have had a nagging feeling that something was not quite right. Having consulted with your doctor, you now know. You're in the early stages of dementia.

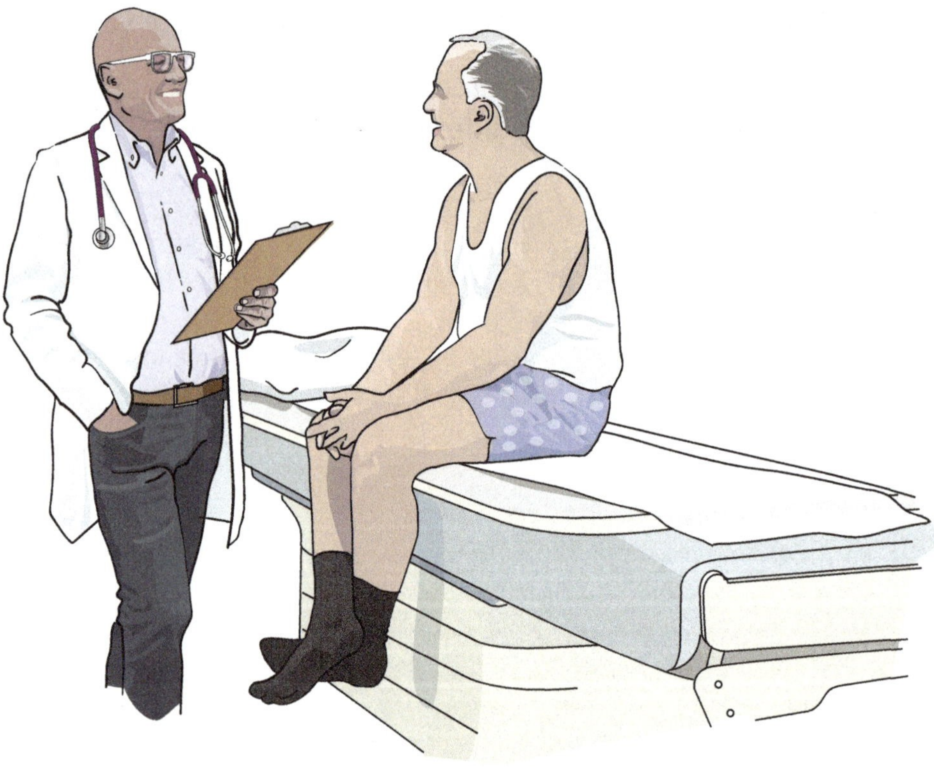

In this stage, you'll be able to continue to do most of the things you always have... most of the time. Most importantly, continue to **ENJOY YOUR LIFE**. Maintaining your independence whether it be at home, at work, or both is still very realistic. The warning signs you encounter will be subtle. These are some examples of the common problems you may start to contend with. Remember, you won't necessarily experience them all, and always, in varying degrees.

Early Stage Indicators

Short-term memory loss

particularly for recent events. You may have isolated episodes when you can't recall:

- Whether you had eggs or cereal for breakfast;
- Why you find yourself in the living room or what you went there to get;
- That you washed your hair three times in one day until someone else pointed it out to you;
- What page you left off in your book or what the story is about.

Personality or behavioral changes

You could find yourself having:

- Sudden, often unprovoked, outbursts of anger, laughter or crying;
- Unexplained feelings of being dejected or blue;
- Moments of apathy about previously important matters;
- Times when you withdraw from enjoyable social situations, even with your closest friends and family.

Being increasingly confused or distracted

You may:

- Keep forgetting what day it is;
- Inexplicably leave the vacuum cleaner in the bathtub;
- Wear a heavy sweater on a hot summer's day;
- Get disoriented or lost

Reduced attentiveness

You might:

- Put yourself at risk by leaving the stove on or the front door wide open;
- Have to be reminded of the rules of the card game that you've played every Friday night for the last few years;
- Constantly interrupt to ask what's happening during the movie you're watching;
- Stop and start whatever activity you're doing until you simply set it aside.

Have trouble expressing yourself

You might:

- Struggle to articulate your point of view;
- Search for common words more frequently;
- Fill in the gaps with words that are out of context and don't fit into the conversation;
- Find people have some difficulty understanding you.

Have lost the ability to perform everyday tasks

You may:

- Strain to align your cardigan to button it up properly;
- Refuse to make the morning coffee anymore because the numbered lines on the pot bother you;
- Wait for someone else to turn on the TV because the buttons on the remote control all look the same and you simply can't get it to turn on;
- Find that the washer and dryer settings prevent you from doing laundry with confidence.

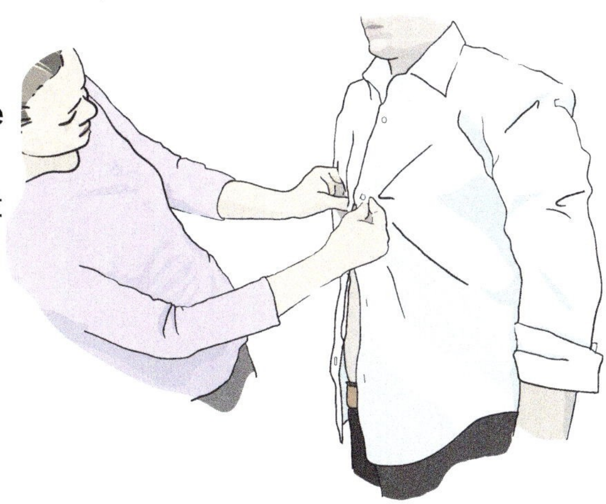

Have problems with abstract thinking

Perhaps you:

- Struggle to understand the measurements in a recipe;
- Have a hard time balancing your chequebook;
- Tell the punch line to jokes before relating the actual story;
- Find common hand gestures that are meant to represent something, say a peace sign or high five, confusing or pointless.

Middle Stage (Moderate)

Many of the indicators listed in the early stage will carry over here. What you'll likely notice is an increase in frequency or intensity. The middle stage of dementia does have some additional challenges and you'll need to prepare yourself for those.

Middle Stage Indicators

Memory loss may now extend to short-term and long-term events

You may have episodes where you:

- Can't remember where you went to high school;
- Start calling everyone in your life "dear" or "honey" to cover up the fact that you can't remember their names;
- Tell your niece that you know she has kids, but you don't really recognize them;
- Order takeout food, but can't provide your address or telephone number to complete the delivery.

Personality or behavioral changes that are more acute

You may:

- Become more argumentative in an otherwise pleasant conversation;
- Fabricate stories to cover up whether or not you are doing things like buying groceries or eating properly;
- Experience false beliefs or delusions, like suspecting your loving partner of 25 years is being unfaithful or that there is an intruder hiding behind the curtains;
- See or hear things that no one else does, like insects in the kitchen, a long- lost friend from your childhood or a menacing character who lurks around.

Being increasingly confused or distracted

You may:

- Suddenly wander off or become lost. When others offer to help you find your way home, you may be unable to tell where you live;
- Find yourself living more in the past - such as interacting with a young child and mistakenly thinking you're their parent instead their grandparent;

- Lose or misplace your things and blame others for stealing them. It may be easier for you to believe it's their fault and not your own;
- Fail to notice or care that you are in public and say or behave inappropriately, in ways that may offend others, like being overtly sexual or using curse words.

Reduced attentiveness that will lessen your ability to do even more things

Someone may tell you that:

- You will need to stop working if the dementia is preventing you from carrying out your work responsibilities effectively;
- You will need to have someone else with you when babysitting young children to ensure their safety;

- You will need to stop taking public transportation to run your errands to avoid getting disoriented or lost..

Have trouble expressing yourself and understanding others

You may notice increased instances where you:

- Have a hard time writing emails, lists, or even short messages to communicate your thoughts;
- Jumble sentence structure and get frustrated because your family can't seem to understand you right away;
- Repeat a word or phrase over and over again when speaking because it feels comfortable and familiar;
- Withdraw from conversation because it's too hard to keep up when several people are talking;
- Lose interest in your favourite movies or TV shows altogether because you can't follow along and get agitated or confused;
- Use more hand gestures to convey what you mean instead of trying to say it verbally.

Have lost the ability to perform more everyday tasks

You may find that you'll:

- Need help with tasks like eating or using the bathroom;
- Need help with housework, cooking or gardening;
- Need notes and reminders posted around the house to help identify things like appliances and their uses;
- Need a cane or walker to help maintain your balance.

Problems with abstract thinking extend to even more basic issues

You may:

- Become increasingly frustrated at your inability to understand or manage your finances, like paying monthly bills;
- Be unable to plan an annual event or birthday party as usual because there are too many details to attend to;
- Look in the mirror and not recognize yourself.

Late Stage (Severe)

Once you reach this stage, most of your physical needs will require assistance from health care professionals and care partners.

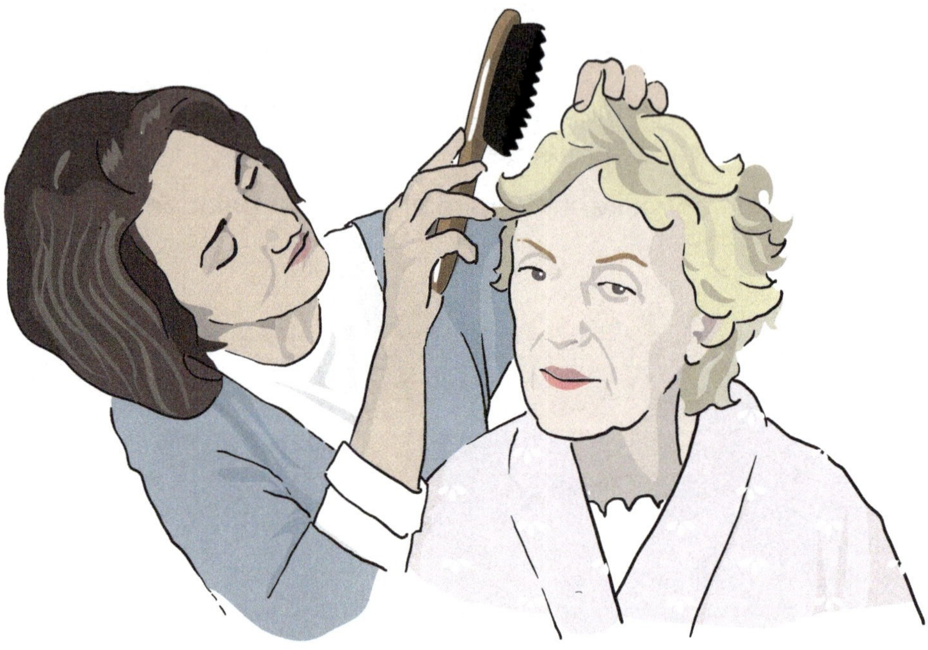

Late Stage Indicators

Though more infrequent, you may still respond to:

- The voice or face of a family member or friend;
- The sound of music;
- The feel or touch of someone familiar.

Physical and psychological needs

You'll likely need help with:

- Basic needs like eating, bathing, using the bathroom, or walking;
- Eating regularly and staying hydrated.

As dementia progresses

You may find yourself:

- Prone to angry flare-ups because you are confused or frustrated at the inability to express yourself;
- Losing control of your bladder or bowel movements;
- Unable to walk;
- Unable to speak;
- Having trouble swallowing;
- Becoming more susceptible to infections like pneumonia or other illnesses.

Regardless of the stage you find yourself in, **focus on what you can do instead of what you can't**. Growth is a continuum in life that does not need to stop because of a dementia diagnosis.

Within any life change - good or bad - exists the opportunity to let go of thoughts or feelings that weigh you down and redirect your energies to the things and people that bring you joy. You have a new reality, there is no escaping that. But with a willingness to adjust, acknowledging where you are right now can bring a surprising newfound peace.

> "Always seek out the seed of triumph over every adversity."
>
> – Og Mandino

Common Causes of Dementia Are Not Necessarily Common Knowledge

No question, dementia is one fussy customer.

Dementia is continuously evolving and therefore, monitoring changes and developing coping strategies will become crucial.

Let's first look at some similar and dissimilar aspects you may come across.

Similarities

What connects people living with dementia together

You cannot have one simple medical test to determine which disease is causing your symptoms.

You will need a series of tests that may include:

- Complete medical history
- Thorough physical examination
- Blood tests to assess such things as thyroid function, cholesterol levels, vitamin levels and more
- Cognitive tests in the form of questionnaires
- Brain scan

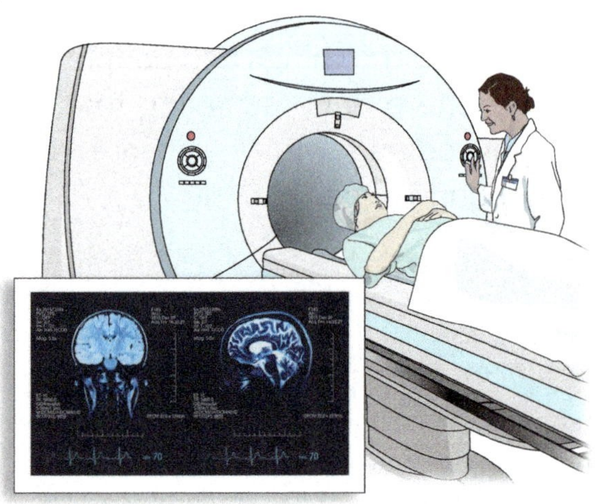

Based on test results, you may then be referred to a:

- Memory clinic
- Geriatric division of your hospital
- Neurologist or other specialists

Many of the diseases exhibit the same symptoms such as memory loss, disorientation, confrontational behavior, apathy, problems with verbal expression and assorted physical limitations. This is one of the reasons why the testing process is so thorough.

You may be diagnosed with more than one type of dementia. For example, if you are diagnosed with Alzheimer's disease and vascular dementia, you then have what is called "mixed dementia".

Your course of treatment is aimed at lessening your symptoms and preventing complications. A comprehensive treatment plan will include recommendations for social stimulation, nutrition, exercise and medications.

You may experience other cognitive or physical conditions that mimic or complement dementia symptoms. These will be addressed further in the next section.

There are some common risk factors associated with the different forms of dementia. These include: high blood pressure, diabetes, physical inactivity or excess weight, depression and limited social contact with others.

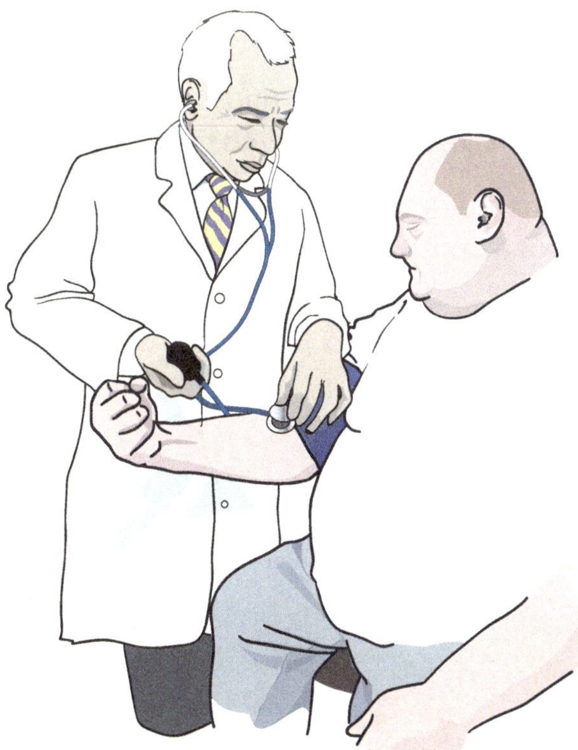

Differences

What distinguishes you as an individual living with dementia

What stage you are currently in and how long you stay there until you move on to the next one.

Any pre-existing medical conditions that must be considered and that may alter natural history and treatment.

Prescriptions and supplements you may already be taking. You want to avoid any harmful combinations that could cause adverse reactions.

Assorted cognitive and physical treatments that you pursue depending on what kind of dementia you have.

Any lifestyle choices you make about exercise, food or alcohol consumption. Your personality, attitude and disposition. This will greatly impact your short-term and long-term reaction to diagnosis and treatment.

Your family dynamic and social circle. These will influence decisions you make alone and with them.

Your culture, traditions and beliefs will naturally inform how you process and move through your diagnosis.

Alzheimer's Disease

Dr Alois Alzheimer

"A peculiar severe disease process of the cerebral cortex."

— Dr Alois Alzheimer, 1906

Some doctors become notable historical figures because they were the first to identify a disease. Coming across an unusual case, Dr. Alzheimer became intrigued and spent over five years closely following and observing a young woman who exhibited progressive cognitive decline and psychotic symptoms.

He subsequently requested a study of her brain. Using his optic microscope, he observed brain atrophy (shrinkage) and two unusual deposits called senile plaques and neurofibrillary tangles, which would become hallmark identifiers of the disease.

You may be asking yourself why, over a hundred years later, knowing this is important. Because that time has given us - and you - a century of learning.

Here's what we know now

The senile plaques and neurofibrillary tangles are made mostly of aggregated or modified proteins, respectively beta-amyloid and tau. These clusters interfere with normal brain activity - like a goalie and defenseman blocking the puck in a hockey game, they purposely get in the way of your memory and thinking. When that happens, it is an indication of the disease interfering with healthy brain cells.

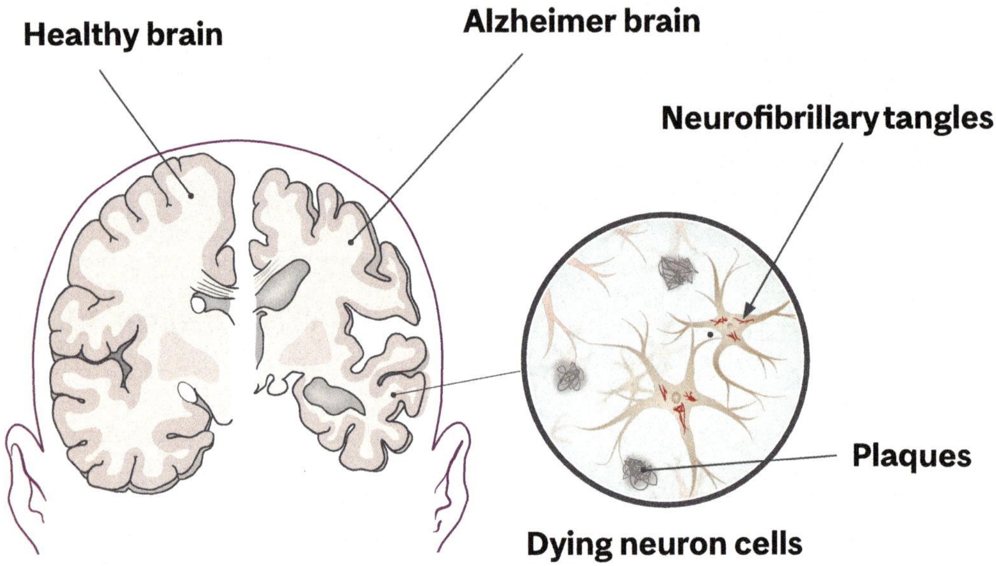

Despite what many people may believe, old age does not cause Alzheimer's disease. Rather, it affects older people at a higher rate than younger people.

You may actually have had Alzheimer's disease for several years before you were diagnosed. Many symptoms can remain outwardly dormant while harmful changes in your brain silently take place.

Symptoms vary from person to person, but usually the first signs are some type of memory loss or out-of-character reactions. You may have attributed this to the natural aging process or brushed it off, probably more times that you care to admit.

Typical responses that tend to reoccur and could indicate Alzheimer's disease include:

"I'm having 'a bad day', everyone does."

– After your son tells you that you've complained about the leak in the garage three times in one afternoon.

"Now I don't know who stole the money! You would be just as frustrated as me!"

– After you missed finding out who the thief was on your favourite TV show because you forgot it was on and lashed out at your partner.

"I don't want to go. I'm tired. We don't have to make such a big deal about it."

– After you've waited impatiently for three weeks for your reservation at your favourite restaurant.

There are other factors that may contribute to the development of Alzheimer's disease. These include:

- High blood pressure
- Family history of dementia
- Physical inactivity
- Obesity
- Smoking
- Excessive alcohol consumption
- Diabetes

Once you start to notice some subtle changes (or someone in your social circle points it out), Alzheimer's disease may continue to alter your memory, thinking, behaviour, and emotions. In the later stages, it may progress to also affect various physical controls over your body.

That said, it is important to stay in the present. It's there that lines of open communication and kindness tends to flourish.

Vascular Dementia

Vascular dementia is the second most common form of dementia, accounting for up to 30% of cases.

The brain needs to be constantly fed by a sufficient amount of blood. Did you know that the brain actually requires about 15-20% of the blood travelling throughout your entire body? This circulation provides the brain with vital nutrients and oxygen, and even removes the waste it no longer needs. When this blood flow is slowed or interrupted, the brain cortex is damaged and brain cells die.

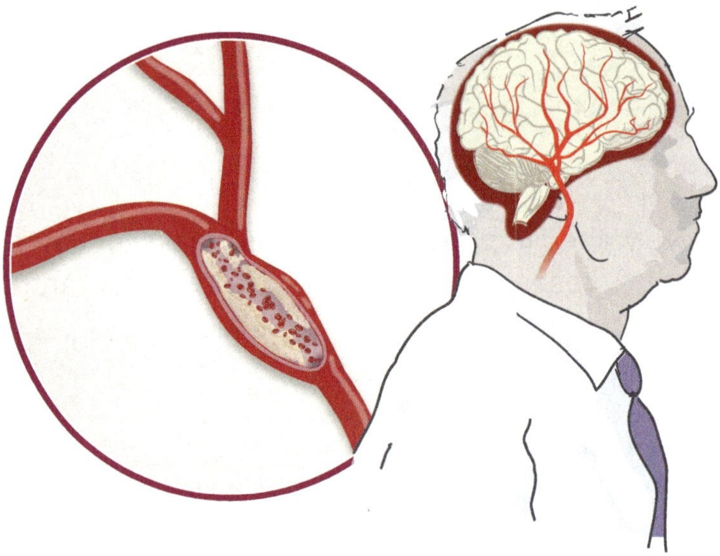

Here's what we know now

Though not limited to it, the major cause of blood flow disruption to the brain is a stroke or a series of smaller strokes. However, it is important to note that if you have had a stroke, it does not automatically mean you will develop dementia.

Vascular dementia is much like a clogged drain in your kitchen sink. Over time, particles of food get stuck in the pipes. Once that food is wedged all together, you'll notice that the water trickles down slowly or doesn't drain at all.

You may hardly notice if you have suffered a small stroke, or even a few of them. Another term you may hear is multi-infarct dementia (MID). This is when a series of strokes build up and block blood flow to particular parts of the brain. Imagine a runaway snowball. It gets bigger the further it slides down the hill, gathering with it memory loss, confusion, personality changes and other symptoms of dementia.

Because a stroke is often a precursor to vascular dementia, this type of dementia can often be diagnosed quickly because the changes in cognitive abilities are immediately observed.

Both Alzheimer's disease and vascular dementia can develop gradually over time, but vascular dementia may also come on suddenly and manifest itself with mild to severe symptoms.

There are other factors that may contribute to the development of vascular dementia. These include:

- History of heart attack
- Atrial fibrillation: An irregular or unusually rapid heart rate
- Atherosclerosis: Arteries that have become thick and stiff and hardened over time, thus restricting blood flow
- High blood pressure
- Diabetes
- High cholesterol
- Obesity
- Smoking

Though vascular dementia will worsen over time, there are treatments, including medication, that can help prevent future strokes and thus additional damage to the brain. You may also benefit from physical, occupational and speech therapies to improve physical conditions such as dizziness, leg or arm weakness, tremors or slurred speech.

Dementia with Lewy Bodies (DLB)

Meet the distinguished Dr. Friedrich Lewy, the namesake of this particular type of dementia.

In his research, he was the first to discover "inclusion bodies". Basically, proteins called alpha-synuclein seek each other out and stick together to form clusters in your brain cells. These invasive structures interfere with the normal functioning of the brain.

Dr Friedrich Lewy, 1949

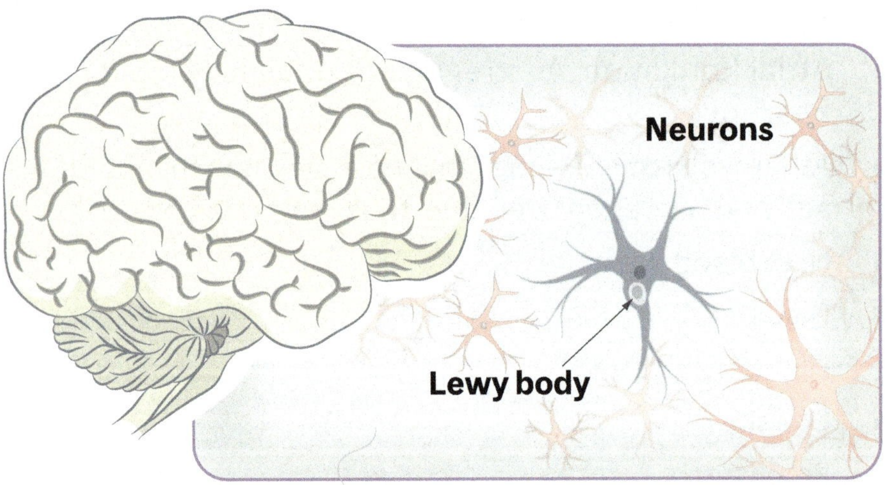

You know how in every group of friends, there's the shy one, the chatty one, the in-your-face one. Well, Lewy bodies is the big man on campus one. He is the overly familiar one that's got to amble over and talk to everybody at the party. That's why Lewy bodies is closely linked with other illnesses. He also likes to maintain an air of mystery. Scientists know less about this form of dementia than the others.

Here's what we know now

Lewy bodies is perhaps the most complex form of dementia as it incorporates many of the symptoms seen in other ailments, notably the cognitive impairments of Alzheimer's disease as well as the diminished motor skills associated with Parkinson's disease. This can make it especially difficult to manage.

There are two types: **Dementia with Lewy bodies (DLB)** and **Parkinson's disease dementia**. Though different conditions, they are biologically related and exhibit the same types of changes in the brain as the dementia progresses.

Given that Lewy bodies model other symptoms so well, obtaining a definitive diagnosis can be difficult. Initially, it can be thought to be Alzheimer's or any number of other psychiatric disorders.

Lewy bodies shares many of the symptoms of the other dementias already listed. However, there are some symptoms that make it distinctive. These include:

Recurring visual hallucinations that appear early in your diagnosis. These false perceptions are usually very vivid and detailed. These delusions could also manifest themselves in the form of physical sensations (hearing, smelling or feeling things that are not there).

Fluctuations in attention and alertness. Levels of consciousness may come and go throughout the day. You may seem constantly drowsy or stare into space for long periods of time.

Declining cognitive abilities such as problem-solving or organizational skills that vary from day to day or even hour to hour. This makes it much harder to track the dementia's progression.

Increased visuospatial problems. This is how we process what we see around us and the spaces and sizes of where we are. You may struggle to get your bearings when walking through a room or outdoors.

You may have rapid eye movement (REM) sleep behaviour disorder. Your dreams seem so realistic that you act them out or talk aloud while still asleep. This is one of the reasons you feel so tired during the day.

Movement disorders. This is where symptoms associated with Parkinson's disease come into play. You may start to move more slowly or experience tremors or twitches, rigid muscles, or begin to shuffle when you walk. These physical symptoms increase the risk of dizziness or falls.

Acting withdrawn or apathetic. It will be hard to regain your sense of motivation when your symptoms are in full swing. This indifference may appear to be depression.

Given the wide breadth of symptoms associated with Lewy bodies, complementary treatments often include:

- Physical and occupational therapy to help with movement problems and to identify viable solutions to everyday needs like bathing and eating;
- Speech therapy to help with speaking and swallowing. These types of exercises will help you strengthen and control the surrounding muscles;
- Given the considerable intensity of a Lewy bodies diagnosis, participation in physical activity, arts or music is strongly recommended to help lower stress and anxiety.

In that same perspective, psychological support is encouraged for both the person with Lewy bodies and their family members.

Finding the right balance of treatment for a person with Lewy bodies requires heightened vigilance. Some antipsychotic medications used to treat hallucinations and delusions may adversely affect motor skills in some people. As a matter of course, your doctor will treat your more severe symptoms first and build from there.

Frontotemporal Dementia (FTD)

Front of the line, front of the class, front runner, united front. In a way, all these concepts stem from using your brain's frontal and temporal lobes.

Your brain can best be likened to a workplace. Every person in the department has a job description outlining tasks to perform. Of course, for an integrated system to work properly, various departments also need to overlap and participate in meetings with open, ongoing communication. All this is done in the hopes of achieving the common goal of efficiency and productivity. Let's take a brief tour of these two interconnected departments that exist in your brain.

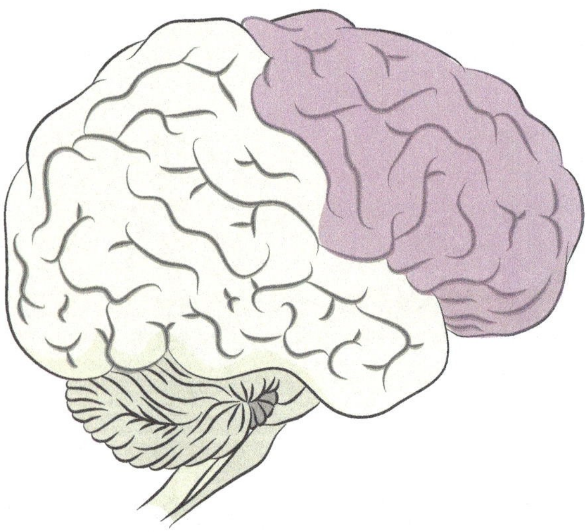

Frontal

Being the biggest lobe at brain headquarters, the workload for the frontal group is expansive:

- Produces speech and language. Basically, it helps put your thoughts into words;
- Coordinates movement like walking or using your arms;
- Helps to generate and keep long-term memories;
- Forms your key personality characteristics; in other words,
- it shapes who you are and how you move through the world;
- Governs empathy, sensitivity and compassion for others;

- Keeps you in check with impulse control, appropriate social behaviour and solid decision-making abilities;
- Keeps you structured by applying planning, problem-solving, reason, judgement and concentration skills.

Temporal

The job assignment here can be divided into three main sections:

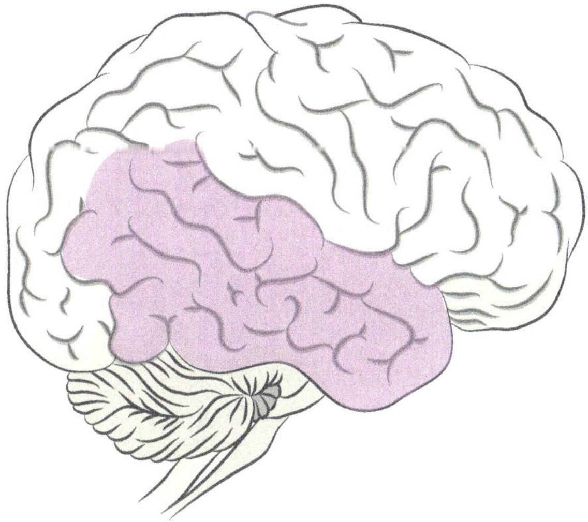

- Interprets and filters the sounds you hear, memories you have and emotions you feel, and gives them all meaning;
- Uses a visual component to make recognition of objects and people possible;
- Understands the symbolic nature of language and conveys meaning so it is comprehensible and can be shared.

Damage to these functions in the form of frontotemporal dementia represents approximately 10% of cases, though it remains one of the lesser-known types of dementia. It is a member of the larger frontotemporal lobar degeneration (FTLD) family. Here, the frontal and temporal lobes of the brain are affected in a two-step process. As neurons die in these areas, the lobes atrophy (or shrink). Located near the forehead, above the eyes and over the ears, changes in your speech, personality, behaviour, impulse control and coordination are usually the first early symptoms.

Here's what we know now

Frontotemporal dementia (FTD) often strikes people at an earlier age than what is generally associated with Alzheimer's disease, vascular or Lewy bodies dementia. In fact, FTD is the most common form of dementia in people under 60 years of age.

It is difficult to get a conclusive FTD diagnosis at first. Early symptoms often present as extreme changes in personality; therefore, it is often misdiagnosed as any number of psychological or psychiatric disorders.

FTD can be divided into sub-types. This is primarily determined by whether the frontal or temporal lobe is most affected. Among the most prevalent are:

- Frontal lobes: Affecting personality and behaviour, namely ***behavioural variant frontotemporal dementia (bvFTD)***
- Temporal lobes: Affecting language skills (word-finding difficulties), namely ***primary progressive aphasia (PPA)***

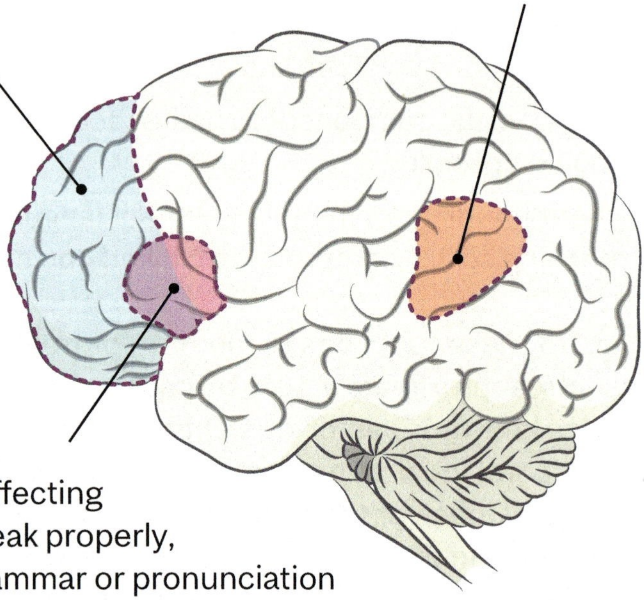

- Frontal lobes: Affecting the ability to speak properly, such as with grammar or pronunciation (progressive nonfluent aphasia) or affecting factual knowledge and meaning of words ***(semantic dementia)***

As stated earlier, dementia can happen to anyone, but FTD does seem to have a stronger genetic predisposition, which indicates that family history may play a larger role in this particular classification.

Unlike Alzheimer's disease, your memory is largely untouched in the early stages of FTD. This is because the damage occurs in these specific areas of the brain.

Though FTD shares many of the previously mentioned dementia symptoms, some that are particularly heightened are:

- Impaired dexterity or mobility for things that require sequential movements, like playing an instrument or dancing;
- Diminished ability to speak, to understand language, or to converse in a way that makes sense;
- Impaired learning and ability to plan effectively;
- Fluctuating mood swings from states of brash social behaviour to restlessness and boredom;
- Downward shift in a healthy appetite, drinking enough water or personal hygiene routine.

After the initial diagnosis, medication and assorted therapy treatments (occupational, physical, speech, vocational) focus on helping you maintain and regain as much functionality as possible. Early diagnosis is key. Then, committing to a lifestyle that spotlights all the good things you can "work" on - nutrition, constructive relationships, enhanced mobility and practical cognitive exercises - makes for an approach that has front-page story written all over it.

Young Onset Dementia

Reaching that middle point in your life where career and family are at the forefront, where self-awareness informs your decisions and where the angst of your twenties is well behind you is a most welcome phase of your life.

There is an inherent freedom that comes with it as well; one that doesn't entertain thoughts of chronic diseases, especially one that targets much older people. Not me, not today.

This form of dementia, however, may affect you before you reach the age of 65. It is rare, on average accounting for approximately 3% of all cases.

Given that, it is understandable that you would discount any symptoms you may experience as something else entirely. However, when you do face the idea that something is wrong, you may wonder whether you are among the select few in this group.

Could it be young onset dementia?

Same symptoms. Regardless of which disease in the dementia family you are diagnosed with, be it Alzheimer's, vascular, frontotemporal or Lewy bodies, the only thing that differentiates you is your age. You can refer to the previous dementia sections to learn about the relevant symptoms and stages.

Delayed diagnosis. Your age may actually delay getting an accurate diagnosis given how uncommon it is. You might have to undergo several different types of tests or doctor visits to narrow down the cause of your symptoms. Possible alternatives your doctor could look for are stress-related issues, menopause, psychological concerns or a specific genetic history.

What you should do

- Maintain or start a healthy lifestyle that includes good nutrition, exercise and a restful sleep.
- Keep doing the things you enjoy - day trips, DIY projects, gardening, painting, crafting, etc. - to help maintain your independence and quality of life.
- Accept help from friends and family - say yes.
- Look for external resources like peer groups or forums (in person or online), therapists, specialized fitness trainers, interest groups or career counsellors to build a solid support system. This can help reduce your anxiety and expand your field of coping skills.

Keep the lines of communication open

- Speak to your employer to explain your situation and discuss possible alternatives to your duties and schedule.
- Speak to a financial planner, as your income may be affected. Major topics to discuss include your mortgage, car, credit card and utility payments, retirement funds and more.

- Speak to provincial and federal agencies to find out what kind of financial support is available to you, such as job and disability benefits.
- Speak to your children to help them understand the changes they may have already questioned and alert them to what they will see in the future. There are books available to help you broach these topics in age-appropriate language. Being aware about what is going on will help make them feel more secure and reduce their anxiety.

- Speak to your partner about how things will change in your relationship. Encourage them to look for external help for themselves to deal with their own set of emotions and stresses.
- Speak to specialists like physical therapists to help with strength and balance or occupational therapists for strategies to maintain life skills, often referred to as activities of daily living. Incorporating such trained specialists into your treatment routine can have a noticeable calming effect on everyone involved. It will feel like you are taking control of particular aspects of your dementia.

Unique challenges you may face

Dementia programs and care are typically aimed at people older than you. This may make it difficult to find suitable resources for someone your age.

Facilities like day centres or long-term care residences may appear well outside your comfort zone, as the services and activities they offer are oriented to the conventional needs and expectations of older people.

Realize nothing is your fault

Yes, it is perfectly natural to mourn the things you used to do without a second thought or the things you'd planned to do, but it can help to focus on what you can do and who you can do it with, realizing that some activities are still well within reach.

Become a dementia encyclopaedia

Surround yourself with supportive friends and family who can help you sort through all the information about dementia. Be sure to use accurate, professional and first-hand sources.

It's not you, it's them

You may discover that the difference young onset dementia makes in your life will make some of your peers treat you differently. Friends, especially those with whom you shared sporting activities, may slowly drop off. The phone may not ring as often as it used to. On the other hand, you'll also discover that those who stay firmly planted in their front-row seats are invested in your relationship and in you.

Sometimes it's hard to sort out the mixed emotions you may have about this unexpected impasse. It doesn't take away any of your shared times or laughter of the past; it simply puts it into perspective for today.

Here are three people who understand and say it better than we could when referencing these friendships:

> "Nothing to say. I'm too busy living the best life I can, with the amazing friends who have stuck around to share it with me."
>
> — Gemma C.

> "I used to miss you but now I wouldn't even know you or me. We both changed and such is life. I have people who get my hurt and still say 'come over when you want.' They see my anxiety and try to steer what is causing it away. Thank you for leaving so I can grow."
>
> — Roxy R.

> "Forgiving you is my gift to you; moving on is my gift to me."
>
> —Unknown

Other Associated Conditions

Subjective Cognitive Impairment (SCI)

No one knows you better than yourself. We all believe that. Like you being the only one who thinks you are having a bad hair day or that red is just not your colour. That extends deeper to knowing what makes you happy or defining for yourself what success really means. It also implies trusting your intuition. So when you start to feel like something has been amiss for a while, you tend to listen to your gut and want to know what is going on.

Could it be subjective cognitive impairment?

It's all in the eye of the beholder. SCI is termed as such because it is based on your own feelings and observations that you are not able to think as clearly, remember names or words as quickly, or plan as decisively as you used to.

Because this condition cannot be substantiated by medical tests, it is considered "self-reported." There is much debate in the research world whether SCI is a precursor to mild cognitive impairment and then dementia. Some contend there is a link to definite changes in brain activity leading to these conditions while others deem it a "benign condition associated with normal aging."

There are some risk factors associated with SCI:

- High blood pressure
- Diabetes
- Physical inactivity
- Lack of mentally challenging pursuits
- Lack of social contact
- Hearing problems left unattended
- Depression

What you can do to help treat SCI holistically

Treat yourself. If you engage in any of the risk factors listed above, make changes at home and see your doctor.

Take your medication as prescribed. This is intended to help you regulate associated health issues, such as high blood pressure. You can also purchase an at-home monitor to track your blood pressure on a regular basis.

Exercise, eat more lean proteins, fruit and vegetables, drink plenty of water and get a sufficient amount of sleep to rejuvenate yourself inside and out.

Make an effort to **reach out** to friends and spend quality time with them.

Play games, watch quiz shows or do puzzles for some brain-boosting fun.

There are many things that can be attributed to your intermittent memory gaps - normal aging, stresses of life, tiredness, vitamin deficiency or being a multitasker with one too many plates in the air. If that is the case, then stop and think about how you can make simple lifestyle changes.

Mild Cognitive Impairment (MCI)

A mild headache. A mild winter. A mild disagreement. In the grand scheme of things, these are not so bad. Even so, you may become curious about your recently developed tendency of forgetting places or names. Like everyone else, you've got a lot going on, so it's no wonder. It's so typical of a multitasker habitually balancing several things at the same time throughout any given day. Yet, when you simply can't seem to wrap your brain around the new software upgrade at work, despite group and one-on-one training sessions, curiosity might give way to mild suspicion.

Could it be mild cognitive impairment?

A name by any other name: Just as it suggests, mild cognitive impairment (MCI) symptoms are slight in nature and should not hinder you from carrying out your daily activities, including work, nor your ability to live an independent life. That is good news indeed.

Two subtypes of mild cognitive impairment have been identified

Though they both compromise your thinking abilities, they diverge in the areas they affect:

Amnestic mild cognitive impairment is the most common and chiefly manifests as memory loss, such as forgetting your lunch plans with a co-worker or searching for your neighbour's name when you start to chat across the fence.

Non-amnestic mild cognitive impairment, on the other hand, is when your learning, organizing, reasoning or judgement capabilities are somewhat challenged.

For example, you may:

- Lose your train of thought during a conversation - "*What was I saying?*"
- Search for the right word to express what you want - "*What I mean to say is...*"
- Become easily distracted - "*Sorry about that, you were saying?*"
- Take longer to complete everyday tasks - "*Right, where was I earlier?*"
- Exercise poor judgement in work or social situations - "*I know it's a meeting but why can't we hug beforehand?*"

You may have one or the other, or both subtypes to varying degrees.

If you've read through the subjective cognitive impairment (SCI) section already and are wondering what the differences are in these conditions, it is that MCI can be assessed and diagnosed by your doctor through a series of medical and cognitive tests. One single test cannot detect MCI. These would include:

- **Cognitive tests** to gauge reasoning, planning and problem-solving skills
- **Medical tests** like blood pressure readings and blood tests to check thyroid function, cholesterol levels, diabetes and vitamin deficiencies or overloads as well as rule out other possibilities like infections

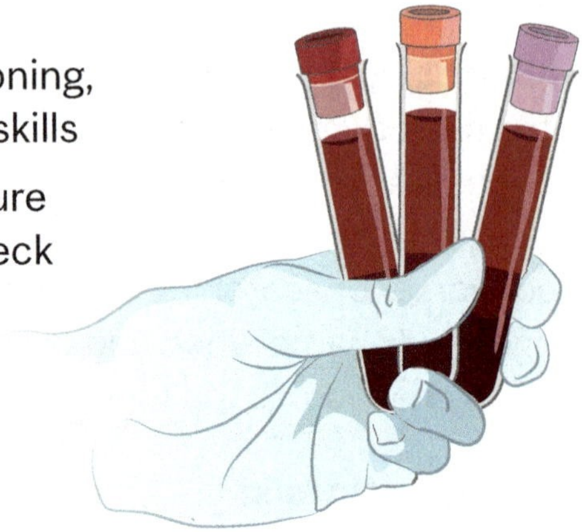

Along with these tests, dialogue and observation are effective indicators to establish MCI. If you have been with your family doctor for several years, they may pick up on some recent behavioral changes. Regardless of having an established relationship or it being your first visit to a new doctor, they will refer to previous notes in your chart and ask you to provide concrete examples of how you feel differently now than before. If someone accompanied you to the appointment, they may also be asked what changes they have come across. Included in the discussion may be topics such as:

- Pre-existing health issues and their current impact
- All medication usage (prescriptions, over-the-counter and supplements)
- Instances of substance use (alcohol, cannabis, sleeping pills, pain medication)
- Capacity to manage everyday activities
- Atypical mood swings
- Memory, language and recognition lapses

Taken all together, your doctor will determine if MCI is indeed the issue and whether an underlying cause makes it treatable.

There are some risk factors associated with MCI:

- High blood pressure
- Physical inactivity
- Depression
- Lack of social contact

What you can do to help treat MCI holistically:

- Adopt a healthier lifestyle including restful sleep, exercise and a diet rich in fruits, vegetables and lean proteins.
- Participate in activities or hobbies that involve other people.
- Engage in pursuits that stimulate you mentally - reading, puzzles, etc.
- Take stock of your environment and make any necessary changes that would make your life easier, more manageable and less stressful.

MCI may change over the course of time

We do not know exactly what causes MCI, but there is the belief among researchers that it may be linked to the same changes in the brain that cause Alzheimer's disease and other kinds of dementia.

That said, MCI does not always lead to dementia. It can remain static or even improve over time. An annual checkup with your doctor to track changes is essential.

Depression

Addressing the very real issues surrounding mental health these days has greatly improved. Due to a concerted effort by associations, health care professionals and the media, there exists a willingness to be more forthcoming and open about this topic. Everyone benefits from this newfound transparency.

It's essential to differentiate a normal ebb and flow of emotions that everyone experiences versus a more frequent state of apathy and listlessness that doesn't seem to go away.

Could it be depression?

People who are depressed may have symptoms that can look like dementia while people who have dementia may seem like they are depressed.

The first step is to visit your doctor to get evaluated as well as rule out any other potential causes of your symptoms, such as a thyroid condition.

Depression is classified as a mood disorder and is usually characterized by these chronic symptoms:

- Prolonged periods of sadness throughout the day
- Indifference for previously enjoyed activities
- Changes in appetite resulting in weight gain or loss
- Irregular sleep patterns
- Restlessness or irritability
- Feelings of anxiety
- Feelings of worthlessness
- Difficulty thinking or making decisions

Physically, you may experience:

- Headaches
- Fatigue
- Aches and pains
- Digestive problems or changes in appetite
- Insomnia or irregular sleep patterns

This combination of mind and body symptoms is considered depression in people with dementia. It is serious when it begins to interfere with your everyday activities and responsibilities as well as your relationships.

Treatment

Treating depression in people living with dementia can include antidepressants. Your doctor will prescribe something that does not have any counter-effects with other medication you may be taking.

Psychotherapy may also prove beneficial as an outlet to express all those feelings. Doctor-patient confidentiality gives you a platform to be completely open and honest.

The combination of the two often has the desired effect of improving the depression and you feeling better.

The world of therapy has opened up to include a variety of approaches including psychodynamic, behavioural, cognitive and humanistic. In fact, there are some unconventional categories such as massage, acupuncture and animal-assisted specialties that can also provide therapeutic support. These could be applied alone or in conjunction with standard therapy, all with the intent to provide you with the tools and strategies to manage your depression symptoms.

No one chooses depression. It is a medical condition. As you enter the later stages of your dementia, getting your motivation up may be a little tougher, even with the positive encouragement of your family and friends.

However, there are still many pleasant things to do to enliven your day such as listening to music or an audio book, being around people you care about, dipping your feet in cool water or sharing a nice meal. **When a door closes, well, just open it again.**

Delirium

There are two conventional ways of looking at and interpreting a state of delirium. One is what many people associate with this word, the context of being "deliriously happy." It points to a heightened sense of excitement not typical of your everyday demeanour. You may find yourself unable to speak or think clearly because of it. The other is when an illness leads to a heightened sense of confusion, again affecting your ability to speak or think coherently. Having said that, when these magnified extremes occur under difficult or demanding circumstances, you have to ask yourself whether the second definition is applicable to you.

Could it be delirium?

Delirium is a condition marked by confused thoughts, a reduced awareness of your surroundings, impaired memory or judgement, garbled speech and acting withdrawn or antagonistically. No doubt these symptoms sound familiar by now. As you can imagine, delirium can often be mistaken for dementia.

However, there are distinguishing characteristics that set delirium apart:

It can start suddenly. The onset of delirium can take hold in a matter of hours or days. Radical mood swings or restlessness are common first indicators.

Duration: Typically, delirium lasts days or weeks and symptoms can fluctuate wildly in intensity throughout the day and night.

Causes: Delirium frequently occurs in people who suffer from the following:

- Previous dementia diagnosis
- Withdrawal from medication, alcohol or drugs
- Dehydration
- Infection
- Previous head injury
- Acute injury or illness causing pain
- Sleep deprivation

It's normally reversible and temporary. Once the source of the delirium is identified and treated, prognosis is usually a near to or full recovery.

Delirium and dementia: People with dementia may have bouts of delirium. Any sudden change in behaviour, as described above, should prompt your care partner to seek immediate medical attention. The sooner you are treated, the sooner the delirium will subside.

Sometimes the answer is simple. Not having access to functioning hearing aids or eyeglasses can lead you to feel disoriented, angry or withdrawn. The inability to see or hear properly would frustrate anyone. If you cannot do so yourself, ask your care partner to check the batteries on your hearing aid periodically and take you to your annual optometrist appointment.

Ways that your care partners can help treat delirium holistically once the primary cause has been determined and treated:

- Use frequent, gentle reminders to situate where you are and what is happening.
- Speak calmly and in a soothing tone.
- Keep you properly fed and hydrated. This will help in your recovery.
- Accompany you doing some form of physical activity. This too will get you on the road to feeling better faster.
- Make your environment as comfortable and familiar as possible should you be temporarily away from home. Family photos, plants or your cozy blanket could help make it feel less intimidating.

Though we often seek permanency in our lives to give us a sense of stability, we can also take heart that some things in our lives can come and go. When correctly treated, most cases of delirium can be a short-lived condition.

Associated Conditions

Alcohol-related Dementia

Enjoying a drink is something that most adults don't give much thought to. Whether it's a glass (or two) of wine with dinner, a beer (or two) watching the game or a fancy cocktail (or two) on a special occasion, getting into the "spirit" of the moment often goes hand in hand with your favourite drink. However, when you cannot enjoy these moments without a drink in hand, without repeatedly reaching for the bottle, it is indeed time to take stock. And if confusion, memory gaps and hallucinations have become habitual consequences of your drinking routine, then you may have to wonder if there is more to it than a simple hangover.

Could it be alcohol-related dementia?

Drinking guidelines. Most governments, including Canada, have outlined standards and limits for what is considered safe drinking practices to reduce long-term health risks associated with alcohol.

Daily alcohol consumption is generally not recommended.

Extreme or binge drinking over long periods of time may induce alcohol-related dementia. This is considered a rare form of dementia.

It is also called Wernicke-Korsakoff Syndrome

Here two syndromes come together and affect the brain and body in different ways.

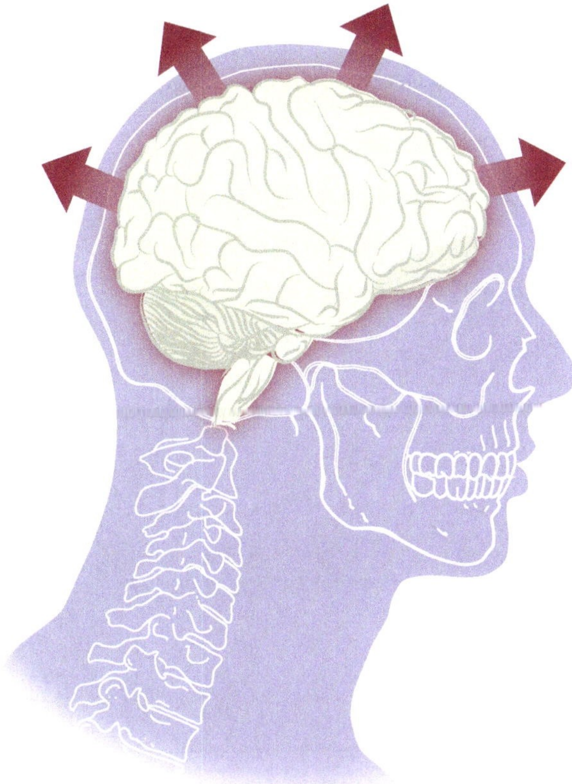

Wernicke's encephalopathy usually precedes Korsakoff syndrome. The abundance of alcohol in your system prevents your body from properly preserving thiamine (vitamin B1) and delivering this valuable nutrient to your brain, causing it to swell and get damaged. Instead of retaining what your body needs, too much B1 is expelled through your urine, leaving you depleted of this needed vitamin. Symptoms include:

- Confusion, disorientation and some memory loss
- Uncontrolled eye movements and vision problems
- Poor balance resulting in an unsteady gait and difficulty walking. This could include tremors.
- Lack of energy

Korsakoff Syndrome evolves from Wernicke's encephalopathy as the next phase, if treatment is delayed. This results in longer term conditions and integrates known dementia symptoms:

- Short-term memory loss
- Difficulty processing information
- Repetitive speech
- Hallucinations

Unlike most other forms of dementia, symptoms develop very quickly and need immediate medical attention. To obtain an **accurate diagnosis of Wernicke's encephalopathy**, tests may include:

- Complete medical history
- Thorough physical examination
- Eye exam
- Gait assessment
- Blood tests to assess liver and kidney function

To obtain an **accurate diagnosis of Korsakoff Syndrome**, some of the same tests will be conducted once you stop drinking for approximately two weeks to establish a baseline of your physical condition without alcohol.

The faster you get treatment, the higher the chance you have of preventing it from getting to the Korsakoff Syndrome stage. In many cases, this situation will land you in the hospital emergency room.

Treatment includes:

- Heavy doses of vitamin B1, perhaps intravenously at first
- Balanced diet rich in minerals and vitamins
- Proper hydration
- Elimination of alcohol - this is the most important aspect of treatment

Professional help: A mandatory aspect of recovering from this condition is that you must quit drinking. You'll need help doing just that. Explore your options with a health care professional, addiction counsellor, support group or all three. If may take up to a year to fully recover. They will be there to bolster your willpower and commitment to make this big change in your life.

The good news

Early treatment can reverse some or most of the symptoms. In addition, you'll most likely see an improvement in other aspects of your life including relationships, job performance and everyday tasks.

Safety In and Around Your Home

One way to take control over your diagnosis is to ensure your home is safe, both indoors and out. Creating an organized, clutter-free and relaxed environment for yourself is important. Maybe for you, it's a place where sweatpants are mandatory and mismatched socks are preferred. There are many things you can do now to set up your space in a way that makes you feel comfortable... and comforted.

Take a look around and consider what you would like to keep the same and what you would like to adjust. Make a project out of it - it'll be quality time you share with your family. It will allow you to keep doing what you want to do and hold on to your independence for as long as possible. It's good for your morale and feeling of self-reliance.

These handy recommendations will also minimize the risk of falls and injury for you and your family.

The *safe* outdoors

Enjoy the lazy days of summer even more by ensuring everyone's safety, especially if your vacation hotspot is in and around your home. If applicable to your home:

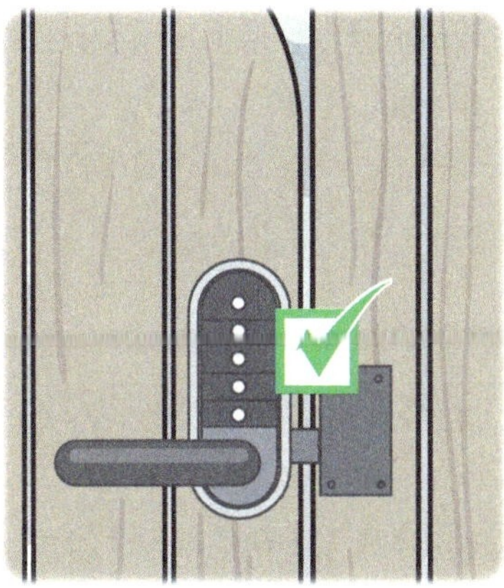

- Set up a safety gate around the backyard and swimming pool.
- Install a lock on the backyard door or gate.
- Keep the grass neatly mowed.
- Trim back any low-hanging branches.
- Mount motion detector lights on the porch or deck.
- Mount motion detector lights on the porch or deck.
- Put in handrails alongside any deck staircases.
- Store tools, gardening supplies and sharp objects out of reach.
- Check for loose pavers, protruding rocks, exposed tree roots or holes that could be tripping hazards.
- Don't leave such things as citronella candles, lanterns, fire pits, or BBQs unattended.

Keep it cool in the winter by having all areas around your home properly shovelled including the driveway, stairs and walkways. You should also:

- Clear away any ice and spread salt or sand on slippery patches.
- Ensure handrails are firmly in place and do not wobble.

Inside the Home

Living room

Add seat cushions to your chair if it is too low; it will make it easier to get some leverage to sit and stand.

Shorten curtains that overflow to the floor.

Arrange the furniture so you can get by easily without bumping into anything.

Look out for throws or cushions that might slip off the couch and onto the floor.

Don't leave shoes lying around, even at the entrance. Put them away in the closet as soon as you walk in.

Remove or fix any tripping hazards like a carpet with frayed or curled edges, and tack down electrical wires.

Look out for sharp edges on furniture.

Kitchen

Check the expiry dates of food in the refrigerator, freezer and pantry. Throw away anything that is past due.

Certain large and small appliances can start a fire or cause injury. These include a microwave, toaster oven, stovetop and oven, even the coffeemaker. Be sure to use appliances that have an auto shut-off feature.

Safely store household cleaners and medications away to avoid accidental ingestion or use.

Safely store away knives, scissors, and other sharp-edged utensils.

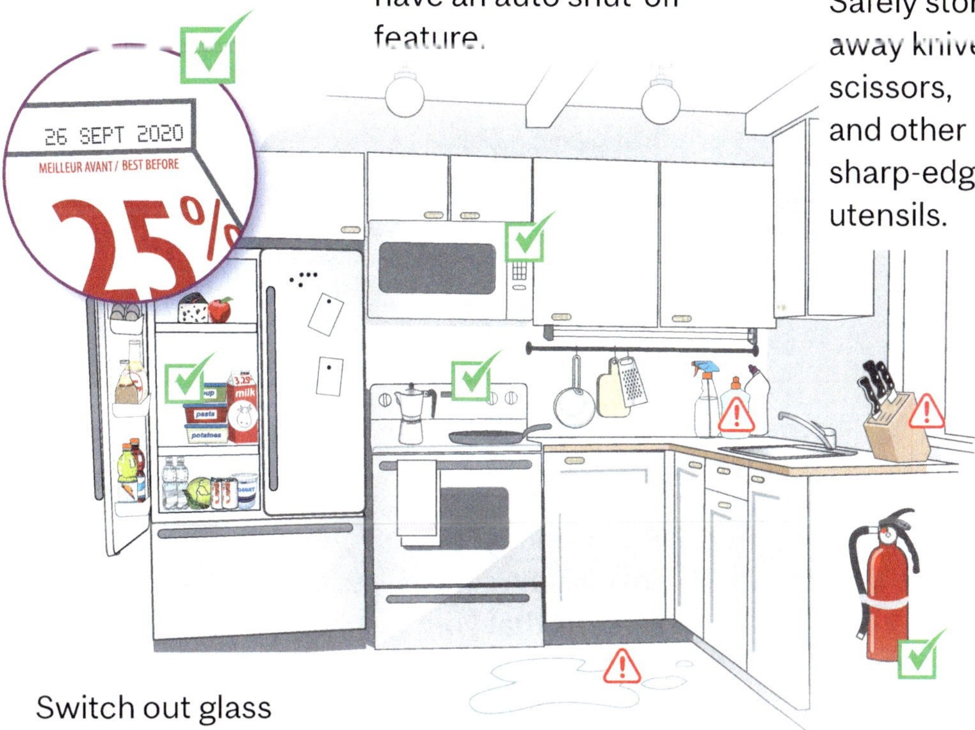

Switch out glass containers for clear plastic ones and label each one. They are lighter in weight and shatterproof.

Don't wear long or loose sleeves around the burners when cooking.

Immediately clean up any water that may have spilled on the floor.

Keep a fire extinguisher easily accessible in a lower cabinet.

If you have one, use a jar opener for those hard-to-open jars and avoid potential broken glass.

Bedroom

Use non-slip socks or slippers.

Place what you may need overnight on your nightstand, such as a water bottle, tissues, throat lozenges, pen and notepad or phone (and charger) to avoid having to get up in the middle of the night.

Ensure there is a clear pathway between your bed, closet and dresser.

Spring cleaning... any time of the year. This may be a good time to go through your wardrobe and decide to donate, store or get rid of things you no longer wear. Once everything is pared down, it will be easier to find what you need and select your outfit for each day.

Think about installing a simple bed rail that you slip in between the mattress and box spring to help you get into a seated position unassisted.

In order to avoid falls during the night, do not leave such things as slippers, clothes, cushions or other objects lying on the floor next to your bed. Avoid keeping throw rugs and pets in the room.

Bathroom

Install wall-mounted grab bars in the bathtub and next to the toilet.

Check out long-handled scrub sponges or loofah brushes to get to those hard-to-reach places.

Install a handheld showerhead. It makes for easier control and reduces unnecessary movement when in the tub. It also allows for you to choose whether to sit or stand when bathing.

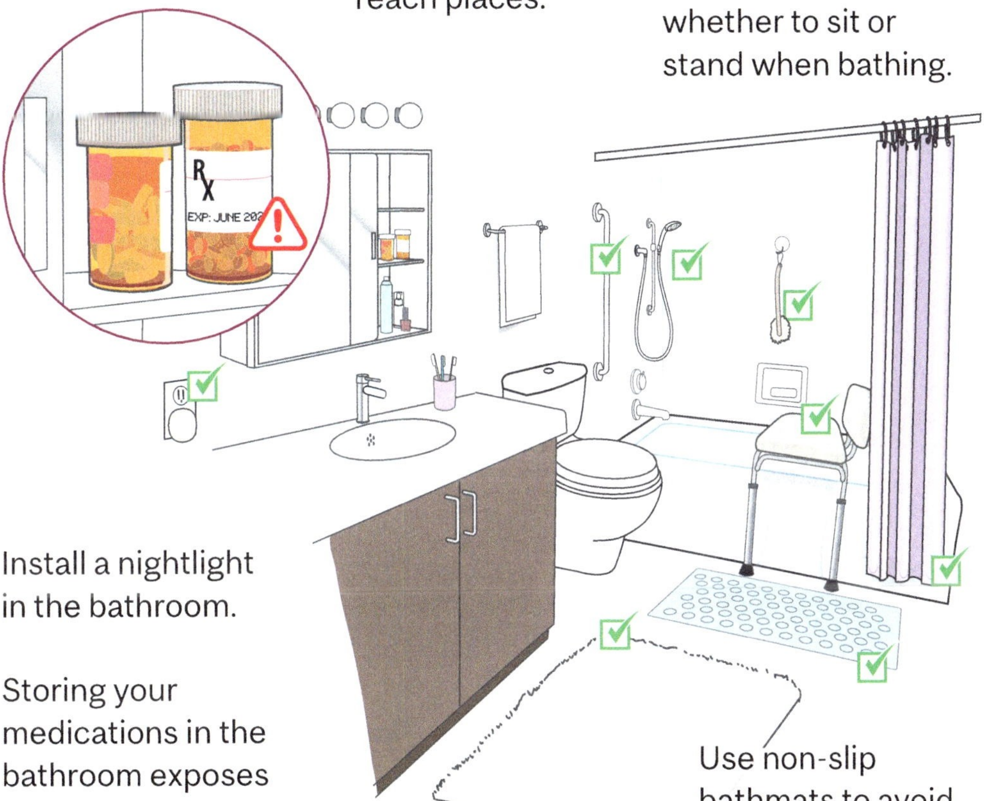

Install a nightlight in the bathroom.

Storing your medications in the bathroom exposes them to humidity. Best to keep them in a kitchen cabinet or bedside table.

Make sure you have a weighted shower curtain to keep water from spilling onto the floor.

Consider getting a bath stool so you can sit comfortably when washing.

Buy some non-slip decals or strips for more traction when standing in the bathtub or shower stall.

Use non-slip bathmats to avoid falling when coming out of the tub or standing in front of the vanity.

General

- Designate drop-off areas for laundry baskets, grocery bags or packages to avoid cluttering rooms and hallways.
- Set all the clocks in the house to the exact same time to avoid confusion.
- Use clear storage containers to quickly identify contents.
- Look out for sharp items one may not necessarily think of, like eye-level metal hooks, knitting needles or decorative items on the console or coffee table.
- Post contact names and phone numbers in large letters throughout the home, such as on the refrigerator, near the front door or on the bedside table.

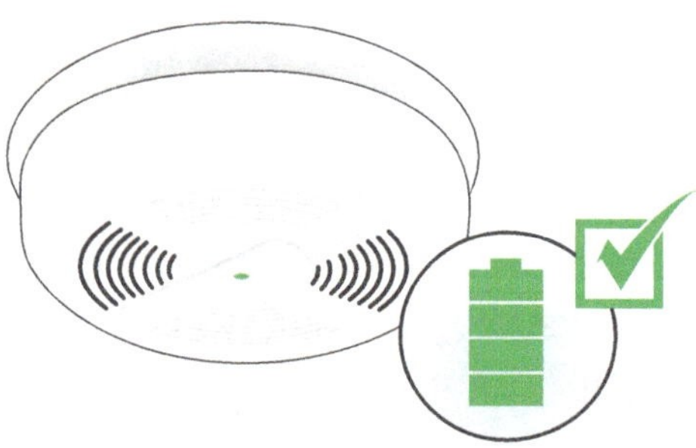

BATTERY

- Ensure smoke and carbon dioxide (CO_2) alarms are well-functioning and check the batteries periodically.

- Have a first-aid kit on hand, perhaps in a couple of rooms.
- Install night lights throughout the hallways.
- Switch from liquid or powder laundry detergents to the convenient single use pods. They are a cinch to use, lightweight and won't spill.

Ask others to:

- Make sure their environment is safe for you to navigate when visiting their home.
- Put things back exactly where they belong after use in your home (remote control, keys, mugs and dishes, etc.).

At the very beginning of this Guide, we said we wanted to take good care of you. Part of that concept is to incite you to take good care of yourself. You know that saying, "It's not all about you." Oh yes, it is.

"I have a relative who I assume has Alzheimer's. This [workshop] has been an eye-opener for me. I recognize that I have much more to learn. "

– Workshop participant, McGill Dementia Education Program

Driving

Nothing provides a sense of freedom like the prospect of driving. It starts when they hand you that 2" x 3" plastic card of independence. And once you start to drive, you don't want to stop. It's a lifetime commitment. That is, until someone says you must stop... and takes away those keys.

Hitting the brakes on driving

Reading signs, anticipating traffic lights, keeping a steady foot on the accelerator or brake pedal and being aware of other cars, pedestrians and cyclists - so many details about driving requires one's full attention as well as good reflexes. Dementia affects these skills as memory, depth perception, psychological and physical response rates may be altered or slowed.

Signs that your driving abilities may be compromised:

- Ignore traffic signs or drive too fast or too slow;
- Neglect to use turn signals or check blind spots;
- Get disoriented heading to familiar destinations;
- Lack confidence and need to pull over frequently;
- Make hazardous driving decisions in the middle of traffic or in designated school or hospital zones;
- Hit the curb or drive onto the pavement frequently;
- Get tickets for improper turns or not fully stopping;
- Mix up the gas and brake pedals;
- Complain that other drivers often honk at you;
- Avoid driving in bad weather or at night.

Once you or a care partner identify any of the above issues, it is your shared responsibility to take the necessary steps to get you off the road.

Deciding to surrender your license

Talk about it with family and friends. **Be an active participant in the decision.** Getting your licence was a significant moment and losing it represents a major change in your life.

Close to home. You may insist that you only drive short distances now, but most accidents occur close to home.

Talk to your health care professional. Physicians have an ethical obligation to report anyone with a medical condition that may impair safe driving. Your medication may also affect alertness and response time and cause drowsiness, dizziness or blurred vision.

Seek out the opinion of a professional to conduct an objective driving assessment, if available.

Check your provincial, state or national policies. These regulate motorist safety and senior driving guidelines to ensure they meet the requirements.

For example, in Quebec, the Société de l'Assurance Automobile du Québec requires that you complete a questionnaire about your health from age 75 onward every two years. This is to ensure a person can safely drive without endangering themselves or others. Your medical history and prescriptions are recorded among any other required tests.

Down the road

There are many other options to get around. The goal is not to keep you tied to the home, but rather to keep you out of harm's way.

These include:

- Taking taxis, ride shares, public or adapted transportation;
- Keeping your car and having others to drive you around;
- Using volunteer driver or shuttle services;
- Asking friends or family to provide lifts. While some outings may be spontaneous, create a schedule for the usual outings, such as trips to the grocery store or shopping centre.

When these alternatives are not readily available, consider online shopping and assorted delivery services.

Wandering

A person can wander in, around, about...or off. Wandering off is a dangerous reality that can adversely affect a person with dementia. Though most often seen in the later stages, it can happen at any time. It is usually an indicator of your declining ability to recognize time, familiar faces or places.

Many things can trigger a wandering episode:

- Thinking you need to keep to your old work schedule
- Overstimulation or extreme anxiety
- Confusion about where you are or where you live
- Trying to find something or someone familiar
- Feelings of boredom or restlessness
- Discomfort or pain, including hunger or thirst
- Side effects of medication
- Pent-up energy from sitting around most of the day
- Trying to relieve joint, hip or back stiffness or pain

You may wander **actively** (seen as purposeful pacing) or **passively** (appearing more aimless and distracted) inside the home. That's okay. However, wandering can be very anxiety-inducing for your care partners when you head outside alone without letting anyone know. You may easily get lost because your sense of orientation is compromised and you may have communication or physical limitations. Your safety and well-being then become the main concerns.

Your care partners can help you by:

- Determining if there is a pattern. Does it happen at a certain time of day or after a particular event?
- Encouraging physical activity to release stress;
- Asking you to help with a household task if they sense you are feeling restless;
- Maintaining your routines to keep nerves at bay;
- Using photos and personal items to create a familiar setting and reassuring you that you're safe;
- Leaving you be if your indoor wandering is harmless;

- Removing visual cues like coats, umbrellas, boots or keys from the entrance.

As symptoms progress and your urge to go outdoors becomes more frequent, your care partners may need to take additional safety measures. **These could include:**

- Locking the doors every time you come in and out;
- Installing a door chime that rings when it's opened;
- Asking you to wear a GPS location device;
- Informing neighbours of your tendency to wander. The more caring eyes looking out for you, the better;
- Preventing it from recurring by figuring out how and why you left;
- Speaking to the other care partners and asking for support, ideas and suggestions;
- Keeping a log of places you like to go;
- Checking on your senior residence's protocols regarding wandering occurrences, if applicable;
- Keeping a current photo of you on hand to share with authorities, if necessary.

It is highly recommended that you register in the MedicAlert® Safely Home® program. This partnership between the MedicAlert Foundation Canada and the Alzheimer Society of Canada has produced a unique MedicAlert bracelet that displays your medical condition and a 24-hour emergency hotline. When calling the emergency number, first responders or police can access your complete medical history and your emergency contact information.

Technology and Other Tools

It's a changing world. Remember when a network only meant which channel you were watching on TV? But then the internet changed EVERYTHING. You know, the queen mother of all networks.

Bringing the world home to you has given rise to specialty markets and products that may have otherwise been unavailable to you. And it has impacted the world of dementia in a big way. There are now many items out there that can make your dementia journey easier, help you maintain your independence longer and minimize your reliance on others. Making some choices for yourself on a daily basis will reinforce your sense of purpose and individuality.

Let's explore

Virtual assistants

These assistants recognize your voice and use your commands to carry out a huge variety of tasks. If you are comfortable using these devices, they can do so much around the house to help simplify your life, like:

Practical services

- Open the garage door;
- Switch the lights on and off;
- Lock and unlock your doors;
- Adjust the temperature, be it heater or air conditioner;
- Create weekly shopping lists for supermarket, pharmacy and any other retail store.

Activities and entertainment

- Available day and night to answer all kinds of questions;
- Tell you the time and indicate what day it is;
- Help plan your wardrobe by telling what the weather is outside;
- Play all kinds of games or even tell you a joke;
- Strike up your favourite tunes or listen to podcasts;
- Help complete a crossword puzzle;
- Set vocal reminders for outings, tasks, appointments or medication schedules;
- Call for meal delivery or takeout - imagine all the new cuisines you could taste.

GPS locators

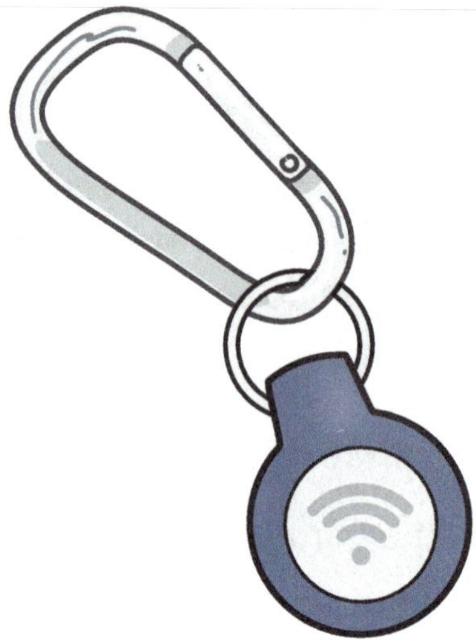

Should you lose your way, these devices alert your family and let them know where you are. If you and your care partners agree to use this type of device, it could go a long way to bolstering your independence and reducing their stress and anxiety when you are out and about.

Item locator devices

Attach a small tile to your most important items like keys, purse or wallet. In case you misplace them, simply push a button on a remote and it will beep to say "Here I am."

Video conferencing

With a few quick clicks on your phone or computer, you can download apps, many free, to start video chatting. This means that you can virtually meet with your doctor, therapist, support group as well as your family and friends. It's the next best thing to being there. And on those days when the weather is particularly nasty or you feel a little extra tired, you'll be grateful to stay home and still keep your appointments.

Other innovative tools to help with everyday life

Walk on by

- Laces tripping you up? Opt for no-lace or Velcro fastener shoes. Ensure they are non-slip and well padded.
- Invest in a long-handled shoehorn to help you get your footwear on without having to bend down.

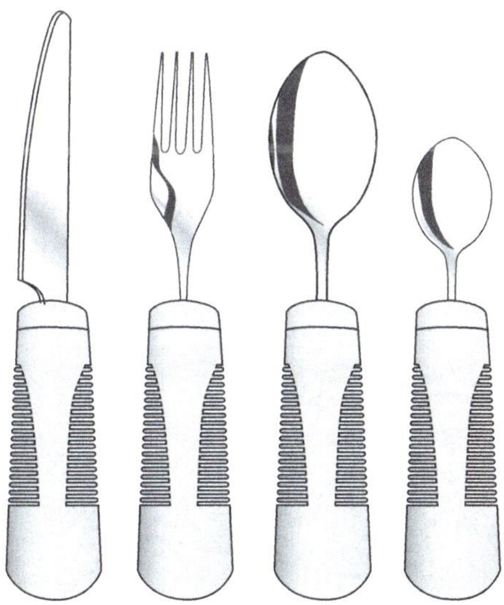

Dinner is served

- Adaptive utensils with non-slip grips and larger handles.
- Dinnerware with non-skid feet to keep plates from sliding around.
- Portioned dishes with high sides to make it easier to scoop up your meal.
- Two-handled mugs.

Right on time

Large font clocks that show more than time. At a glance, they also display the day of the week, full date with month and year, and even period of the day like morning, afternoon or night.

Go big at home

- Large-scale wall calendars
- Big button remote controls
- Magnifying glasses
- Large and colourful pill dispensers
- Big button telephones that light up when you get an incoming call
- Telephones with amplified sound to ensure you never miss a call. Some also have a noise reduction feature to eliminate all the unnecessary background sounds.
- Full-size signs to post on doors to identify rooms
- Realistic oversize pictures indicating the contents of cupboards or closets

Dress for your success

These tips will help make you more self-sufficient with this daily ritual and ensure you don't neglect it. And, you get to add some new items to your wardrobe for that "feels like me" style:

- Opt for loose fitting tops with no buttons or zippers. It will simply be a matter of slipping it over your head.
- Use tie-on belts to avoid the nuisance of a buckle.
- Complete your look with colourful scarves that you can easily drape over your shoulders or around your neck.
- Opt for boxers instead of briefs.
- Try front closure bras because they are easier to get on and hook up the enclosures.

At your fingertips

Keep items that you use daily or weekly in your lower cabinets or drawers for quick, unaided access.

There's no question that ground-breaking technology in general as well as specific inventions aimed at providing everyday health solutions will improve your life in many ways. And adopting easy, practical tips will take some of the guesswork out of daily situations. Embrace their positive features and make them work for you.

Proactive Planning

> "Someone's sitting in the shade today because someone planted a tree a long time ago."
>
> – Warren Buffett

Planning is a good thing. **Planning for the unexpected is what makes for a good plan.** Things may not go as expected; people may not behave as anticipated. And you need to be prepared for that.

Be Prepared

Anyone can suddenly need to leave home when faced with an urgent situation. Putting together a kit with some necessities would allow you to react quickly without forgetting something essential. Using waterproof bags to keep items dry and secure is an extra precaution you may find useful.

This kit can include:

- A change of clothes and shoes
- Extra keys, glasses, hearing aids and medications
- Copies of financial, legal and insurance documents as well as care partners' contact information
- Snacks, bottled water and essential toiletries

Financial and legal protection

Taking the time to plan for your financial and legal protection in advance will provide you and your family with peace of mind. Several documents exist to ensure that your requests are carried out.

Power of Attorney

This document only refers to property and authorizes someone you trust to carry out assorted day-to-day financial tasks such as paying monthly bills, the rent or mortgage. It authorizes the person to make bank transactions in your name, such as withdrawing or transferring money. Though you may still be able to make these decisions, the power of attorney authorizes one or more of your care partners to handle these matters while you focus your energies on your well-being. This document must be notarized to be valid.

Banking regulations vary throughout the country, so if you are considering creating a simple power of attorney at your bank, you may want to check with your local branch to ensure this is feasible. Though this may be easier, a notarized power of attorney is still preferable and recommended.

Will and Testament

Once someone passes, a will is the official record that states how you want to distribute your assets. Making a list of your property (house, items in the home, savings, etc.) and debts (mortgage, loans, credit cards, etc.) simplifies everything when the time comes to settle your estate.

Again, every region is bound by their own laws. Check out local government sites for questions about the various acceptable legal forms a will can take. If possible, consult a notary or lawyer to benefit from legal advice and avoid any confusion that could lead to conflict among family members.

Practice good planning by gathering and storing away all important papers in one place and informing a trusted care partner of the location. This should include bank account and credit card numbers, insurance policies, investments, loans or pension plans.

Protection Mandate

This official document gives you the power to decide who will act and speak on your behalf, if and when incapacity makes you unable to do so for yourself. Incapacity can happen to anyone, at any age, at any time. While still of sound mind, you can choose one or several people you trust, called mandataries. For example, you may appoint two or more siblings, children or grandchildren. In fact, you can even assign what each mandatary takes care of, such as daily well-being, medical options in the event of incapacity, or even the care of minor children.

Every province, state or country has its own requirements for the creation of a mandate and what is needed for it to be considered legally binding. Refer to the appropriate local government websites. These may even have sample mandate forms to guide your efforts.

Advance Medical Directive

Also called a living will, this informs your family and health care professionals of your medical care choices when you cannot speak for yourself and are incapable of consenting to care.

Financial Abuse

Financial abuse is an unfortunate and all-too-common outcome of having a long-term health condition. Some think that dementia makes you more vulnerable, and thus, easier to manipulate. Seniors with pensions, property or disposable funds are especially targeted. Protecting yourself and being vigilant is key.

Regrettably, most abuse is conducted by individuals you know well who purposefully exploit your relationship. They may have access to your money or documents and make unauthorized financial transactions or take items without your consent.

Though organizations are usually staffed by honest and trustworthy individuals, there may be some within their ranks who are deceitful. Thus, some informal or professional care partners, representatives from various retail locations or institutions with direct access to you may say they want to help but their intent is to cheat you.

Finally, strangers with fraudulent schemes may approach or contact you with the aim to financially exploit you.

Any person in one of these groups can pressure you to take out a loan, sell, transfer or give away property or money, or fail to deliver on paid items or services.

Signs that there may be financial abuse:

- Irregular spending, unexpected activity such as cashing in long-term investments or valuables suddenly gone missing;
- Unpaid bills or the inability to access accounts;
- Someone isolating or controlling you. Your family may be genuinely concerned, especially if they witness psychological abuse such as bullying you into making transactions;
- Someone suddenly acting like your new best friend after your dementia diagnosis.

Sadly, people who seek to abuse will take advantage of factors associated with your diagnosis, like faulty decision-making, struggles with complex subjects, forgetfulness, loneliness and dependency on others, in order to manipulate you. Share your concerns with other trusted care partners or your health care professional so that appropriate action can be taken.

Scammers

While technology has certainly made some aspects of our lives easier, it has also made it easier for scammers to operate. That's because our contact information is so readily available to anyone around the world. Imagine it like a stranger walking through your front door without being invited. You can be contacted by phone, text, email or post. As a person with dementia, and with support from your care partners, there are steps you can take to help prevent this from happening to you.

- Make financial arrangements with your bank. This can include making a care partner a co-signer on your accounts. It's another set of eyes to monitor banking activity and help you navigate your financial needs.
- Set up direct deposit for incoming cheques and automatic withdrawal for monthly bills.
- Establish limits on debit and credit cards.
- Have some cash on hand but protect yourself by keeping this amount reasonable.

You and your care partners must pay attention to red flags. Never provide personal information, send a cheque or transfer money to someone you don't know. This is a common tactic fraudsters use to keep you hooked... and to keep stealing your money.

"You can have more than one home. You can carry your roots with you and decide where they grow."

– Henning Mankell

Where to call home after a dementia diagnosis

At times, the best decisions are the ones that apply to situations that have yet to happen. Another aspect of being **a good planner is looking ahead to the future**. The evolution of your living arrangements through your dementia diagnosis is one such situation. This cycle may include staying at home, moving in with a family member or moving to an assisted living facility.

Staying at home

Home is where you can be your true self. It's your safe place and everything is set up as you like it. With dementia, an important goal may well be to preserve your independence and stay home for as long as possible. The goal of your care partners' circle will revolve around ensuring that you stay home safely.

Speak to your family and friends as well as health care professionals to define your initial needs. Only small changes and limited support may be required at first.

That said, **you and your care partners should be proactive** and reach out to private and community organizations as well as regional, provincial or national government health agencies serving your area. These can provide appraisals and home-based support for lifestyle, nursing, fall prevention and personal care services to complement support offered by your family and friends. Much of this will be dictated by where you live, how many people can lend support and the availability of services in your community.

Moving in with a family member

When your symptoms increase to the point that living at home is no longer a viable option, moving in with a family member may be an alternative. Discuss the suitability of this step beforehand as part of your plan.

This is a weighty decision, one strongly motivated by love and kindness, though one that could greatly impact many people. Your care partner's spouse and children may not be entirely receptive to the idea. The additional responsibilities, the constant presence of external care providers and the changes to their home life may be too emotionally or physically draining. Consult with health care professionals and experienced care partners to get a realistic picture of what this may look like for each person.

If you decide to move forward with this choice, encourage your care partners to schedule respite time for themselves and social activities for you. This dual tactic will help ward off loneliness and isolation as well as contribute to **everyone's overall mental and physical well-being.**

Moving to an assisted living facility

Here is where taking advance initiative will truly serve you and your care partners well. There may be several assisted living facilities available, and with that, a multitude of factors to consider. These could include:

- Costs
- Convenient location
- Dementia-centric services and appropriate internal policies
- Cleanliness
- Safety and crisis protocols, including medical emergency readiness
- Professionally trained staff
- Daily events and activities to stimulate social interaction
- Availability of medical staff such as doctors, dentists or physiotherapists

- Onsite amenities such as a hairdresser, pharmacy, place of worship or bank as well as pleasant outdoor spaces
- Guidelines and restrictions regarding visitor
- Healthy meals that can be adapted to special dietary needs. Can you eat in the communal area as well as choose to have your meal in your room?

Depending on your location and whether you select a public or private facility, there may be measures in place when you request a file be opened in your name. This may include meeting specific criteria, reviewing which places best suit your needs as well as an evaluation of your physical and mental functions. As the aging population grows rapidly, there may be established waiting lists.

You and your care partner(s) are strongly encouraged to tour a couple of facilities to get a feel of the place, staff and fellow residents. This will minimize unwanted surprises and prepare you for what to expect. Above all, you'll want the residence to feel safe and comfortable.

Any of these moves is a major life adjustment. You may experience stress and a sense of loss. Your care partner(s) need to be sensitive and patient while acknowledging that the unfamiliar surroundings and new people will require time and effort for you to accept.

People Living with Dementia - Self-Care

Every few months, a new buzzword comes along that captures everyone's attention. Most fade from our lives rather quickly. However, one in particular is here to stay.

It's self-care.

It's not to be confused with:

Self-assured
OR Self-esteem
OR Self-made
OR Self-aware
OR any of the many concepts that have adopted the "self" prefix to secure their place in our world.

Given our heightened focus these days on both physical and mental well-being, self-care is more than a movement, it's become a way of life for many. The problem is... what exactly does it mean? **And what does it mean to you as a person living with dementia?** It's one of those boundless concepts that mean different things to different people. So many, many different things.

When it comes to people living with dementia and their care partners, self-care cannot be an afterthought but rather must be a necessity.

Communication

The most important thing you can do for yourself in terms of self-care is to communicate. Especially at the beginning of your diagnosis. That voice inside your head that you sometimes ignore - and sometimes think is positively brilliant - it's time to really listen to it.

Think back to a time when you were sitting on a plane and it hit some turbulence. The number one instruction they give you is to put on your own oxygen mask first before helping anyone else. **That's self-care. And at this moment in your life, is there anything more turbulent than your dementia diagnosis?**

> "The first step toward change is awareness. The second step is acceptance."
>
> — Nathaniel Branden, Psychologist

Between you... and you

The one thing you cannot do, unfortunately, is go back in time and reverse your diagnosis. **It's OK.**

You'll go through a wide range of emotions. **It's OK.**

There is much to learn about your diagnosis. You will have to apply yourself so that you can make informed decisions about today and tomorrow. It will go a long way towards easing your anxiety. **It's OK.**

Some days, your coping skills will be on point and carried out with amazing confidence. Other days, you may stand still and feel unproductive. **It's OK.**

You may change your mind over and over again about how you want to handle things. **It's OK.**

You will have good days. You will have bad days. **It's OK.**

Despite this diagnosis, know that your life can and will be fulfilling, joyous and worthwhile. Make that conscience choice for yourself every day.

Be kind to yourself.

Between you... and everyone else

It's OK. You're human. And luckily, there are other humans out there to help smooth out life's bumpy roads. A sense of belonging and security can be found in a variety of places along your dementia journey.

Friends and family

Talking about your diagnosis and all that it will encompass with those closest to you will be difficult, but in an odd way, also heart-warming. At first it will be an opportunity to share your feelings and your apprehensions about the future. Opening up to the people you trust the most will provide some **much-needed reassurance.** It will also be time for you to express your gratitude and love for their presence in your life.

The truth of the matter is, the realization will come that these people, the ones you value most, may become your care partners. These are relationships that need to be nurtured because they will be tested repeatedly as your dementia progresses. This will not be an easy journey... for you or for them.

You need not tell everyone in your life at the same time, as this could be overwhelming. Pick and choose who and when. You may even decide to have someone close to you inform some people outside your inner circle of your situation to avoid too many emotional or possibly awkward situations.

Take steps towards **attaining peace of mind** as you move forward with your diagnosis. This is an essential element of self-care to take into consideration. To achieve it, you may need to have some difficult conversations along the way regarding your legal and financial affairs or the type of care you want as the dementia progresses.

Being on board with the decision-making process and ensuring that what matters to you is carried out will ease the burden for yourself and for your friends and family. Clear and precise documents will take the guesswork out of the equation. No doubt you will feel like there are certain aspects of dementia that are out of your control, but this need not be one of them. **Here is where you can feel powerful instead of powerless.**

Your diagnosis may also be an **opportunity to let go of negative emotions** you may have pent up over time. Why still feel guilty about getting promoted over your co-worker when it was not your choice? Why stay angry at your best friend because she didn't call you right away about your son's acceptance to college? Why hold on to jealousy because your partner likes some innocent flirting? Letting go of these useless emotions is as much about self-care as anything else.

You're facing the unknown. There is no right or wrong way to react, process or accept. But make sure you react, process and accept.

Pro tip

You may want to think about seeking professional help. The world of mental health has changed plenty in the last few years. Speaking to a psychologist, psychiatrist or therapist is an additional resource at your disposable to help maintain your emotional well-being, especially if you are in need of someone trustworthy to confide in.

Advantages include:

- A safe place to be yourself and voice your innermost thoughts;
- Someone who can devote their full attention to you without distraction;
- An environment of non-judgemental listening;
- Helpful counsel and strategies that will better equip you to deal with your diagnosis.

Strength in numbers

You may also want to join a support group. No one can really understand what you are going through except another person who is going through it. These groups can provide you with:

- A great source of information and inspiration;
- An opportunity to ask in-depth questions about what living with dementia is really like;
- A chance to learn about resources and services you may otherwise be unaware of;
- The possibility to bond and form friendships with people who "just get you".

Three Stations of Care

Work it out

There are three steps, or stations if you will, to help you attain self-care status during your diagnosis. These are tips and suggestions to think about, to get you started on something and hopefully to incorporate in your daily or weekly routine to continue doing **your best to live your best life.**

Cognitive Station - Think Positive

There are lots of ways to help focus and stimulate your mind - and the best part is they are fun to do. Nothing says you cannot enjoy life during this time. Is there a long-abandoned hobby you would like to take up again? Want to try something completely new? **Now is the ideal time to make time for yourself**. Here are some suggestions:

- Play board games.
- Learn a new language.
- Read.
- Play video video games.
- Do crossword puzzles and word games of all kinds.
- Write - creative writing, journaling your dementia journey or sending letters to your friends and family.
- Take up a new hobby - knitting, model cars, gardening, etc.
- Plan trips to the museum or library.
- Treat yourself to something you've always wanted.
- Draw.
- Meditate.

Physical Station - Body Language

Let's start with the basics, what we like to call **SEE.**

Sleep well
Eat properly
Exercise regularly

These basics are the foundation of good health for everyone. For you, they can work in concert with your prescribed medications or physical therapy. The stronger you are, the stronger you'll feel for what is ahead.

Did you know that being active can help relieve some of your stress as well as promote regular sleep cycles? There are lots of other pleasurable things you can do to give your body some needed attention:

- Take a bubble bath.
- Get a mani/pedi.
- Indulge in a massage.
- Go apple or strawberry picking.
- Go bowling or go to the mini-putt range.
- Get a haircut - it's a guaranteed pick-me-up.
- Go dancing (even if it's in your own living room).
- Take an afternoon nap - is there anything better!
- Take a walk around your neighbourhood or out in nature.
- Take a fitness class like yoga, stretching or aqua fitness.

Social Station - Reach Out

Staying connected with your family and friends has so many benefits. Fun for one - and who doesn't need a healthy dose of that? Your mood and outlook will sometimes waver. That's to be expected. But surrounding yourself with people you love being with and who love you will certainly help that. So fill up that social calendar with some of these ideas:

- Sunday brunch with your friends;
- Zoom or FaceTime sessions - there's nothing like seeing a smile;
- Board games or card games - make it a regular thing with friends or grandchildren;
- Cooking - decide on a cuisine and dish up some new favourites;
- Baking - chocolate. Need we say more?
- Community activities - book clubs, painting classes, etc.

Self-care doesn't have to be time-consuming

Lest you think self-care is just one more thing you have to worry about, there are also some quick and easy things you can do to make time for yourself:

- Enjoy a cup of tea or coffee in a quiet corner of the house.
- Watch the sunset for a while.
- Listen to your favourite music for 15 minutes.
- Read just one or two articles in your magazine.

In essence, incorporating self-care into your life is taking control. Quality of life is not handed to you...or anyone else for that matter. You have to create it. It has everything to do with how you see yourself while you deal with this diagnosis and the decisions you make about how you want to travel its path.

What do you see?

Summary

A dementia diagnosis does not define ALL of you. You can continue to enjoy a fulfilling life.

Dementia is not one disease. Rather, it is a group of symptoms that happen because of a disease. These symptoms manifest through cognitive impairments and decline. Basically, dementia accelerates the natural changes that an aging brain undergoes.

Dementia is the loss or destruction of nerve cells and their connection to the brain. When that connection is skewed or lost, your thinking, behaviour and feelings become affected.

Age is the leading contributing factor to developing dementia.

Dementia is progressive. Symptoms will increase over time. This applies to both your physical and mental states.

Not every person will exhibit the exact same set of symptoms leading to their diagnosis and even throughout their illness.

Dementia is an equal opportunity syndrome that can happen to anyone. It does not discriminate based on gender, economic status, sexual preference, geography or ethnicity.

There are three sequential stages to dementia: early, middle and late. Each stage has its own set of symptoms and challenges.

The common causes of dementia are Alzheimer's disease, vascular dementia, dementia with Lewy bodies, frontotemporal dementia and young onset dementia. While most will exhibit similar symptoms, there are some crucial differences.

There are several other conditions that may appear to be dementia. They include subjective cognitive impairment, mild cognitive impairment, depression, delirium and alcohol-related dementia.

As dementia affects your psychological and physical response rates, your driving abilities may be compromised. You may have to decide to surrender your license for your own safety as well as the safety of others.

Wandering off is a dangerous reality that can adversely affect a person with dementia. Several measures can be taken to ensure your safety and physical well-being.

Technological advancements and innovative products can make your everyday life easier to manage and help you retain your independence longer.

Financial abuse is all-too-common for people with a long-term health condition. Protecting yourself and being vigilant is key.

Technology has made it easier for scammers to operate. Consult your trusted care partners and your bank and take the appropriate steps to prevent this from happening. Refrain from sharing personal information or sending money to anyone you don't know.

Creating a home environment that is safe will help prevent the risk of falls or accidents as well as set the tone for a stress-free environment.

Actively incorporating self-care routines, both physical and psychological, into your daily and weekly life will provide reassurance, peace of mind and a sense of control over your diagnosis.

Section II: Care Partners

A Care Partner Journey Leads to a Prescription in Education and Support

I have been in your shoes. I was my mother's care partner for 12 years. That experience shaped who I am today. I am telling you my story because I don't want it to be your story too.

My mother was diagnosed with Alzheimer's disease in September 2006, and this, on the heels of a tumultuous period. My father had recently died, and I'd just given birth to my third child after a difficult pregnancy. I had a job, a husband, a home and society's expectations of me. And now I also had this - becoming a care partner. And I needed to be the best care partner ever.

People who knew me back then were never able to break through the Superwoman persona I had created long before. I was impenetrable - fortified with a suit of armour and one remarkable superpower. A deep-seated belief that I could handle it all. That is, until I couldn't.

Adding the unyielding daily reality of managing my mother's care as I was confronted with so many peculiar cognitive symptoms and demanding physical challenges did me in. I was completely unprepared for how hard and confusing it was going to be.

I cracked. I cracked wide open. And I did it to my "self." I self-medicated with alcohol and self-soothed with online shopping. I was self-righteous in my demeanour and self-indulgent in my choices. I became self-destructive in how I handled my own personal health as well as my relationship with my children and husband.

I had care partner burnout. I was depleted and had nothing left to give myself or anyone.

In retrospect, I got there for two reasons. One is because of who I am. I've always placed unrealistic expectations on myself to excel and surpass. I hid my vulnerability as a human being to meet everyone's expectations of who I should be - perfect - and what I could do - everything.

The other reason is because my mother's diagnosis left me completely unprepared.

"It's dementia, good luck." That was the entirety of the medical counsel I received. Dementia is complex and the medical community doesn't always provide enough information, nor do they emphasize the importance of pursuing educational or community services, two vital support systems needed to take the best care of the person with dementia. Families are rarely given a "prescription of care" to rise to the challenges associated with this condition. Throw in the lingering stigma attributed to dementia, preventing many from seeking the help, and you end up with a "prescription for trouble" instead.

I got help. And I was lucky to be surrounded by people who cared about me. During this healing period I became a volunteer mentor, then a certified dementia care consultant. A guest lecturer spot at McGill University led to an invitation to launch a pilot project to educate family care partners.

If this kind of support had been available to me, my life may have gone in a different direction. By then, I knew I wanted to help those who came after me to be better informed about dementia and its considerable impact on everyone involved.

Remember, your primary objective is to ensure that the person with dementia is HAPPY, SAFE AND WELL LOOKED AFTER.

Here's what I learned.

ACCEPT THE DIAGNOSIS. That's the only way a person with dementia will receive the best care. Due to their brain trauma, they may experience anosognosia, or the inability to recognize that something is medically wrong. So, it falls to you to push past the initial shock and their rejection of it. 106

ACCEPT THE SUPPORT. "Many thanks, but I'm not there yet." I cannot tell you how many times I have said these very words or heard them from other care partners over the years. Why is it that family members feel they can't ask for support nor have the right to live their own lives? Dementia has a ripple effect. Taking care of yourself from the start may ward off a crisis later, like burnout, that would negatively impact everyone, including the person with dementia.

Build a care partner circle immediately after diagnosis - family, friends, community and/or private and public resources - to help with tasks, and to provide mental health and respite support.

EDUCATE YOURSELF: Knowledge is your most powerful tool. Learn all you can about symptoms and progression. Ask lots of questions. Research support services in your community. Use this Guide as one of those tools.

ANTICIPATE: Dementia changes constantly, so you need to stay one step ahead. Making decisions about health care, personal needs, living arrangements, legal and financial matters is crucial. I strongly recommend that you and your loved one do this together while still feasible.

NAVIGATE: Accessing public and private programs can be a lengthy process, especially if high demand creates waiting lists. Again, start early to obtain the best possible results at the right time for you.

ADVOCATE: The role of advocate became one of my most important. This safeguarded my mother's well-being and dignity for the remainder of her life. I became her voice, and you will have to do the same for your loved one. Making life choices for someone else is profound; file it under the header "tough love." Remember, your primary objective is that they remain **HAPPY, SAFE AND WELL LOOKED AFTER.** Let that be your guiding force.

All these topics are addressed in detail in this Guide. We have made strides since my mother's diagnosis, and we will continue to forge ahead.

Me and my mother, Vieno Leskinen, Montreal, Quebec, April 2015

Sending all of you best wishes for resilience and strength.

Claire

Claire Webster
Founder & Ambassador,
McGill University Dementia Education Program

Dementia and Care Partners

The diagnosis is confirmed and a new commitment between you and the person with dementia will unfold. You will face unexpected situations and challenges but there will be one constant. Dementia will evolve and change over time, and so will your relationship and responsibilities.

Though this is a different perspective, you are travelling that same road together and the curves that lay ahead make it hard to see at times. But continuing to put one foot in front of the other is the most important part of this dementia journey.

To help you do just that, Section 2 is full of tips, recommendations and strategies with one goal:

To develop a shared language and understanding and build a solid relationship between you and the person living with dementia. This will be the framework that shapes how you manage the diagnosis together.

We recommend that you also take the time to read Section 1, which is addressed to the person living with dementia. The more you know, the better equipped you will be to contend with what is ahead. You'll gain a better insight of the specific type of dementia the person you will care for has been diagnosed with, and learn what to expect throughout the three stages of the syndrome.

That said, Section 2 is intended for you, the care partner. It is presented in a practical way to help you:

- Determine what type of care partner you are;
- Manage your emotions and expectations;
- Find practical tools to cope with various situations;
- Develop effective communication skills.

Finally, **learning to prioritize your own well-being** while you care for someone else is crucial. We'll provide you with ideas and suggestions on how to take care of yourself.

There may be hurdles, misunderstandings, and yes, some bad days, but it does not have to define every aspect of your life nor that of the person living with dementia. While this Guide aims to prepare you for the challenges, it also intends to remind you that there will be joy, laughter and affection. You'll learn how to redirect your focus from what can no longer be done to what can. **No one is defined by just one thing. And dementia is just one thing. It does not speak to all of a person and everything that makes them unique.**

The journey starts. And this Guide will accompany you every step of the way.

> "Like all individuals, people with dementia are people first. Like all of us, they have an inherent dignity, value and personhood which remain with them throughout the whole course of the disease, and this needs to be respected at all times."
>
> – Alzheimer's Society of Canada

It begins.

So, something happened.

Did you get an anxious phone call

from your best friend?

Were you all asked to come to your parents' house?

Are you remembering all those odd conversations with your partner?

And is that why you're sitting there, huddled together in anticipation?

Is someone going to say it's dementia?

Care Partner Defined

Words matter. That's why the definition of care partner is so important to understand and why we are using it here in our Guide. Care partner evolved from the often-used term "caregiver." This suggests an imbalance in the relationship where the person with a condition assumes a more passive role.

In their broadest sense, both terms mean providing someone assistance and support with the tasks of daily living. Whether it be because of failing health, age, accident or fall, mental illness or in this case, a dementia diagnosis.

Identifying as a care partner instantly conveys cooperation and connection - **partners in care.** Here, the focus will be on friends and family care partners - people not paid to actively participate in the day-to-day life of a person with dementia.

Dementia calls for big doses of empathy and patience. Much will depend on the type and stage of dementia, your relationship with your loved one and its dynamics as well as your own family and work situation. As you can imagine, it will alternate between frustrating and rewarding, sad and joyful.

As stated in the first section, dementia is progressive. It can also be unpredictable. That means any strategy or solution that worked one day may not necessarily work again. Being able to adapt and change course will be essential. This inevitably includes learning from your mistakes as much as from your successes. There will be both.

You do not have to do this alone. Relying on others in your life will be invaluable to both you and the person living with dementia. Throughout this section, we'll list a variety of resources you can reach out to for assistance and support.

Types of Care Partners

Every care partner circle is different. Often, care partners are spouses, partners, children, siblings, nieces or nephews, close friends and even neighbours. Any combination of the care partners described below can be put in place.

Primary care partner

You provide daily support in a variety of ways, be it physical, psychological or emotional. It can range from managing the household, cooking and cleaning, assisting with bathing, dressing, eating and medication, or accompanying them to doctor's visits and other outings. You'll also help with vital decision-making and provide a compassionate ear to listen to the needs and concerns of the person you are caring for.

Secondary care partner

This person is typically considered a back-up resource to the primary care partner. They may alleviate the load in the evenings or weekends, run errands, or help with any other tasks. There may actually be several secondary care partners.

Long distance care partners

Care partners who live far away can still help. They can access online resources or make phone calls to set up appointments, pay bills if authorized, and arrange for cleaning, yard work or meal delivery services. All of these initiatives are important and help lessen the load. They can also provide emotional support to other care partners and the person with dementia through regular phone or video chats.

Professional care partners

If you have other responsibilities such as a job or children of your own to care for, finding a balance between your needs and the person diagnosed may be helped by having someone qualified come into the home to assist with everyday tasks or provide companionship. You can explore both public and private options in your area.

Informal care partners

There may be a host of care partners within your network... think of them as a village. Caring neighbours who mow the grass without being asked, a friend who takes you out for dinner or a volunteer who spends time with the person diagnosed with dementia.

Ongoing discussions will be needed among you all to determine which partner role you assume and how to divvy up the tasks. This should be based on your availability, resources, abilities or talents. These will be ever-changing depending on the dementia stage and symptoms.

> "The oak is the strongest tree in the forest, but the willow bends and adapts. When the fires and storms hit, it is the willow that survives."
>
> – Kara Barbieri

Becoming a Care Partner

Friends and family are usually the first to notice that someone's forgetfulness or odd behaviours are becoming more frequent. This should prompt a visit to a health care professional for answers and **may well be the start of your journey as a care partner.**

Don't be put off by your their denial through remarks like:

> *"Of course, I remember her. It's just been a while."*
>
> *"I'm tired, that's all. It'll be better tomorrow."*
>
> *"I misplaced it again. No need for dramatics."*

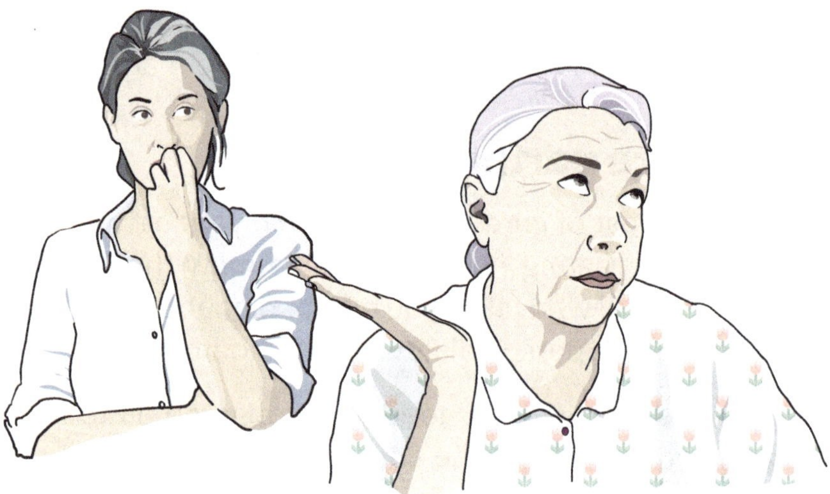

Few words have the power to completely turn your world upside down like dementia. Important facts to retain:

- This diagnosis is irreversible.
- Impaired reasoning, judgement and personality changes are significant markers of dementia.
- Problematic behaviour, offensive words or actions are often the result of dementia's effect on their brain. Your loved one is not being purposely difficult, lazy or rude. Try not to take this personally.

Acknowledging Your Emotions

Much like there are stages of dementia, there are stages of emotions in the face of this diagnosis. No one responds the same way or in the same order. **The only consistent thing you can count on is that it will be different every day.**

You may experience any of the following:

- Abandonment and denial as someone important to you will undergo life changes beyond anyone's control;
- A natural wave of empathy, compassion and sadness;
- Frustration, anger and even guilt as you contemplate how this diagnosis will interfere with your own life;
- Anticipatory grief as someone you admire or depend on for companionship and love will progressively be lost to you. A reversal of roles can be hard to accept;
- Dismay and resentment if your relationship was complicated or fragile before the diagnosis. You may have a negative attitude that will be tough to overcome, or see it as an opportunity to heal a fractured relationship;
- Longing for how things used to be. You'll yearn for moments from your shared past that were meaningful.

You are entitled to all your thoughts and feelings. None are wrong and there is no place for judgement here.

Communication

People living with dementia don't remember that they can't remember. That's something you have to remember.

The very nature of dementia affects the ability to organize thoughts and to speak them out loud.

Communication is how we reveal who we are, what we be lieve in, and what makes us happy or sad. It is how we share our ideas and stories about our past and present, as well as our hopes and aspirations for the future.

It's also how we learn all these things about other people. That exchange is what makes us connect to one another.

There is a learning curve for everyone involved in this diagnosis. As a care partner, it will test you, but if you let it, it could be an enduring life lesson that confronts your own fears - and embraces your courage.

> "I've learned that people will forget what you said, people will forget what you did, but people will never forget how you made them feel."
>
> – Maya Angelou

Verbal Cues

Though this may be obvious, verbal cues are revealing. However, to be an effective communicator, **it's more than just the words you say, it's how you say them.**

When combined, the following elements of speech can relay such things as interest or disinterest, confidence or uncertainty, empathy or anger. When communicating with the person with dementia, be aware that these will impact your exchange and how your message is received.

Timing: Adjust your speaking pace to emphasize key words so that the listener can absorb and reflect on what you are saying.

Volume (loud or soft): Maintain an even tone of voice and avoid shouting.

Pauses (length of pause, how many): Avoid rambling on and using too many fillers such as "ums" or "uhs."

Tempo (speed, be it fast or slow): Speak slowly and pronounce words clearly to ensure understanding.

Intonation (rise and fall of a voice): This is the rhythm of your voice and can express emotions. Avoid a monotone delivery that can transmit boredom.

Adopt these useful techniques:

- Always face the person and stay in their sight line.
- Use verbal affirmations like *"I see"* or *"I understand."*
- Ask open-ended questions first, such as *"What can I do to help you?"*
- When these become too challenging, switch to closed-ended questions that only require a *"Yes"* or *"No"* type of response or choice: *"Do you want to wear the blue sweater or the green one today?"*
- Keep rephrasing questions as needed: *"The blue one?", "The green one?"*

- Tell them what you are doing as you do it. Narrating what is happening can be soothing and shift the mood from tense to peaceful.

- Duplicate what they say to show you understand them: *"So you're telling me that..."*
- Use short sentences and repeat as often as needed.
- Give clear, concise instructions and refrain from giving too much information at one time.

Being a good active listener

Though you may be well-intentioned, hoping to meet their needs quickly, being patient will not always be easy. Typically, it will take a person living with dementia longer to make themselves understood.

Avoid these poor communication habits:

- Interrupting. Anyone would get irritated if they were constantly cut off.
- Speeding conversations up by filling in gaps. Allow the person with dementia enough time to respond.
- Providing your own interpretation of what they mean before they have a chance to complete their thought.
- Making snap judgements or impulsive responses.
- Correcting or contradicting when their memory of a person or event is skewed.
- Using idioms or expressions that can confuse, such as *"speak of the devil"* or *"break the ice"*.
- Being patronizing, talking down or talking over a person with dementia. Always be respectful.
- Distracting noises, such as a loud TV or radio, high-spirited children or pets in the same room.

The truth is, the needs of a person living with dementia come ahead of your own when establishing how to communicate effectively with one another. Their understanding of what is happening around them and being understood takes precedence. One way to avoid potential conflict is to make an important decision: any behaviour that is not harmful to themselves or anyone else - **just let it go**. Keeping stress at bay will always be a benefit to everyone.

Non-Verbal Cues

There is an abundance of scientific research that indicates that we humans "talk" to each other in a variety of ways that does not include the actual words. Some studies suggest that it is approximately

70% while others go so far as to attribute 93% of communication to this category. Non-verbal communication never stops. It includes facial expressions, eye contact, body language, posture, touching, sounds and how close you stand or sit next to someone.

Remaining engaged and friendly improves the chances of a productive exchange.

Tips to communicate successfully:

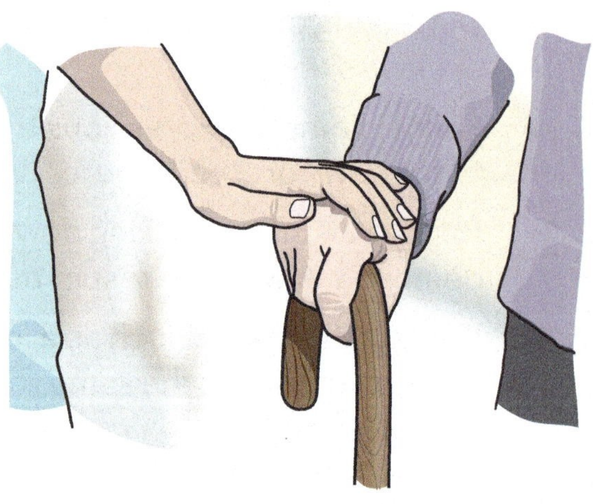

- Use a pleasant voice. Don't yell out to your loved one from another room.
- Maintain eye contact and say their name often.
- Provide comfort and affection through gentle touches.
- Avoid repetitive actions that trigger adverse reactions.
- Become comfortable with periods of silence.
- Ensure your words align with your non-verbal cues.
- Use gestures to emphasize your meaning. For example, point to the towel and shampoo for bath time.
- Validate their emotions. Everyone, dementia or not, wants to know they have been heard.

- Refrain from eye rolls, pursed lips, frowns or foot tapping to replace verbalizing your impatience.
- Avoid getting verbally upset with them. Step away for a while to collect yourself, if needed.
- Laugh as often as you can. Humour heals, connects and releases tension. All good things.

Adapting your tone and facial expressions will become important skills to learn as the dementia progresses.

While adapting your communication skills, it is equally important for you to be attune to how and what your loved one is trying to convey to you.

They may be trying to tell you that they are:

- In physical pain or discomfort;
- Bothered by loud noises or bright lights;
- Hungry, thirsty, bored or lonely;
- In need of the bathroom or tired and want to go to bed;
- Wearing uncomfortable clothes or shoes;
- Too hot or too cold.

Additional tips

Check their vision and hearing

Schedule annual checkups with the optometrist or audiologist. If applicable, ensure their glasses or hearing aids are working properly.

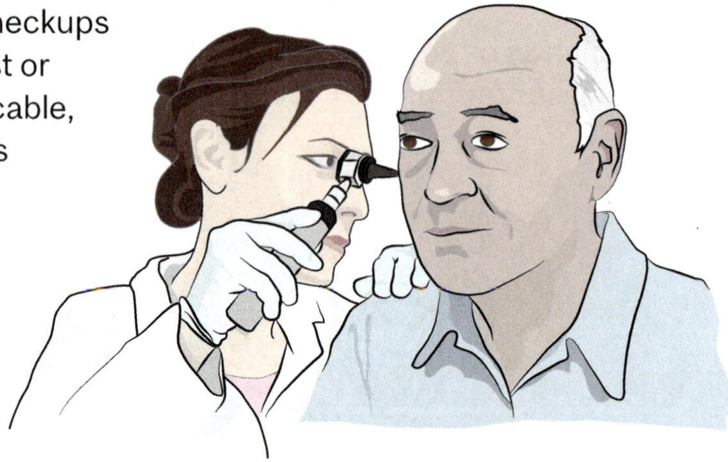

Fill their space with a scent they enjoy

Stimulate their senses with a favourite perfume, flowers, linen spray or freshly baked goods.

Watch TV together

Select programs they enjoy or find relaxing. Nature shows, comedy or romance are a good bet.

Read out loud together

Pick a beloved book or author. Even the latest gossip magazine could be an amusing diversion.

Play music

Pick a favourite genre, singer or band. Listening to music they don't like may have the opposite effect.

It takes work for any life relationship to be successful. As a care partner, devoting extra energy to understand verbal and non-verbal signals will help solidify your bond and trust. That said, no one is perfect. You will most likely experience your own moments of boredom or hostility. Forgive yourself. Tomorrow is another day.

Navigating complicated personal dynamics

Whether it's the family you were born into or the one you choose, there are many great things about being part of a family - love, friendship, belonging and acceptance. They are your truth tellers, critics, mentors and peers. They're home.

However, when faced with a situation like dementia, conflicts and tension can arise. You each bring your own set of values to the table and that may create a buffet of emotions that tests the care partner circle.

Each family member may:

- Process and acknowledge the diagnosis differently.
- Interpret the definition of "care partner" differently.
- Determine what the right "solution" is differently.
- Approach communication about the topic differently.
- Allow their differing relationships with the person with dementia and with each other to influence decisions.
- Let sibling rivalry, jealousy, resentment or favouritism resurface and have differing points of view.

In other words, everyone has baggage. This is uncharted territory and how you all navigate the waters will be different.

Tips on how to reduce conflicting viewpoints

Call a meeting and involve the person with dementia. This is feasible when in the first stage of their diagnosis. Have your loved one take centre stage to express their preferences about their care, who is involved, the family home, outside assistance or anything pertaining to their diagnosis. Though more difficult in the middle or late stages, you can still make the effort to acknowledge their requests.

Ensure everyone respects the wishes of the person with dementia as much as possible. This could initially align everyone's efforts. Hopefully, you all agree that you want the best possible care for your loved one.

Keep everyone up to date to avoid resentment or hurt. Allow everyone to have their turn to respond uninterrupted.

Shared topics could include:

- Results of the latest doctor's appointment and what new treatments may have been recommended;
- Comments made by the person with dementia regarding their needs or concerns about the condition's progression;
- Costs incurred due to legal, financial, medical, or home-based expenses;
- Suggestions for hiring a professional care partner, nurse handyperson or cleaning service;
- Transitioning the person from their home into a residential or long-term care facility.

Accept what you cannot change. Don't waste time and energy arguing. Nothing is absolute and given the nature of the syndrome, things evolve constantly, including how everyone adapts to the situation.

How to make responsibilities fair among partners

The reality is, you probably can't. **Someone will always step up and do more** and assume the role of primary care partner. It may depend on the type of relationship, physical proximity, finances, who can incorporate the care into their schedule better and who can emotionally deal with the complexities of caring for a person with dementia.

That said, **be precise with requests for help**. Create a list and distribute it to everyone. Have them take the lead and select the tasks they want to take on. Review and adjust the list on an ongoing basis. Be flexible and accommodating. If you are alone, look into local social services that can provide assistance.

Establishing Routines

We all approach day-to-day life differently. Are you a worshipper of routine or a chaser of the spontaneous? When it comes to being a care partner, **opt for routine every time**. It will help you structure your week, day or even your hour, as well as provide a reliable schedule for the person with dementia. Less guesswork and more preparation will often lead to the desired outcome.

Streamline information among care partners:

- Invest in a **hard cover agenda** to note daily activities. Discuss with your family members and get their input.
- Explore multi-person **online calendars.** Use it to delegate tasks, cut down on individual texts, emails or calls and streamline information.
- Create a **group text chat.** This is a quick way to signal any last-minute changes or to ask a question.
- Create an **email distribution list** to collect everyone's contact information. This can also be used to share more substantial document attachments.
- Set up an **online video conferencing group.** Schedule weekly chats to exchange information, swap days or tasks based on availability.

- Set up **face-to-face get-togethers.** Do it over a meal for some real-time contact and support in a more relaxed setting. It's a morale booster and safe space to vent with the people in your circle.
- **Grab a coffee**, that other essential food group. Schedule short video calls during break time.
- **Build trust**. Be open-minded to other's opinions and commitments. At times, you may have to say "No" as well as accept "No" from someone else. Create space to make that OK.
- **Follow through as much as possible.** Stick to the "mean what you say and say what you mean" philosophy. If you are relying on each other to keep all the plates spinning in the air, you cannot disengage or back out of responsibilities too often.

Tips to simplify a routine for the person with dementia

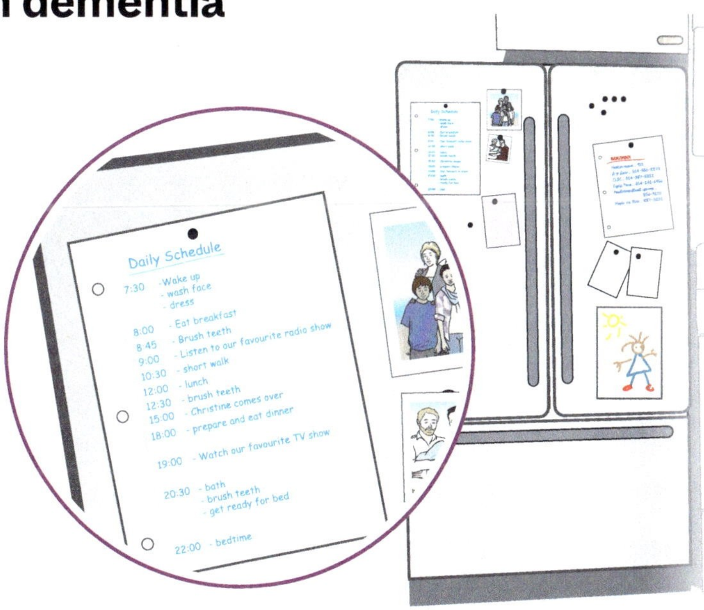

Schedule the same tasks at the same time every day. Knowing what to expect and when creates stability and promotes a sense of accomplishment for the person with dementia when done successfully.

Setting daily goals and following defined steps taps into their internal clock. Like most of us, a person with dementia tends to wake up, eat, exercise, and sleep at relatively the same time. People with dementia may hold on to that memory reserve for a long time and find routine comforting.

Know their habits. The more involved you are in their daily activities, the more attuned you'll become to their ways. Maybe they like to eat breakfast before getting dressed or they like to brush their teeth before they shower. It will make them feel in control, minimize stress as well as show them that you respect their choices.

Be considerate. When helping with personal routines, you both may experience embarrassment. No one anticipates that they will need assistance with the mundane tasks of putting on their clothes or washing their face.

Helping a person with dementia is about improving their quality of life by encouraging their self-confidence and independence for as long as possible more than it is about picking out the right shoes or sweater.

Dressing

Looking good is feeling good, whether it's your best fancy outfit or that cozy loungewear set.

Tips on making it easier for them to "dress the part":

- Ask them what they're in the mood to wear.
- Suggest an outfit based on activity or weather.
- Set out their clothes in order of what goes on first, starting with undergarments, socks, pants and top.
- Pick out two options and let them choose.
- Combine verbal and non-verbal cues like pointing to the closet and saying, *"Let's pick something to wear."*

- Encourage them to do as much as possible on their own before you step in to help: *"You got it."* Maybe they only need to be buttoned up.
- Help them in small, measured steps. Pass them one article of clothing at a time with clear instructions for each: *"Slip your arm right in there."* Don't rush them.
- Remember that you are there to help, not supervise. Don't assume an imposing stance or dictate the process.
- Affix pictures and labels on dresser drawers to show what is inside such as "socks" or "pajamas." You can point to these to help them pick out the items.

- When they select clothes that don't match, let it go. It doesn't matter all that much.
- If they are willing, help them go through their closet and remove any items they no longer wear. Decluttering will make the dressing routine simpler.
- Remove out-of-season clothing from the closet to avoid squabbles, like wearing a coat in the summer.
- If you lack room, divide the closet into seasonal sections. Use garment bags to keep winter clothes out of sight during the summer and vice versa.

Grooming

Grooming is like your own personal pick-me-up. Who doesn't feel better with freshly washed hair, a shave or a swipe of your favourite lip colour?

Boost their mood using these tips:

Reinforce a positive image by giving sincere compliments: *"Your hair looks great parted on the side like that."*

Make grooming a special outing when possible. Schedule appointments to the barbershop or salon. Combine cues by pointing to their face or hair with a supportive statement such as, *"It's Friday morning, time to get even more beautiful."*

Consider using at-home grooming services if going to these places causes more anxiety than happy anticipation.

Grooming times two. Imitation is the sincerest form of flattery, they say. If appropriate, comb your own hair, clip your fingernails, brush your teeth or apply some eyeshadow alongside them as a daily encouragement: *"I'm doing it too."*

Familiarity breeds comfort. We all have our preferred soaps, creams, shaving mousse or aftershave. Keep to the brands they know. Engaging their senses may encourage them to keep up with their grooming practices.

Make eye contact and then gently guide their hands when increased symptoms make it harder to follow through on such tasks. Be their cheerleader. Say: *"Look at that great smile"* while helping with brushing their teeth.

Tell them exactly what you're doing: *"I'm going to bend down now to slip your leg into the pants."*

Explore online sites for helpful tools when decreased mobility becomes an issue. These include nail clippers with a non-slip base, adaptive toothbrushes, blow dryers with attached brushes or electric razors for care partner use.

Additional tips

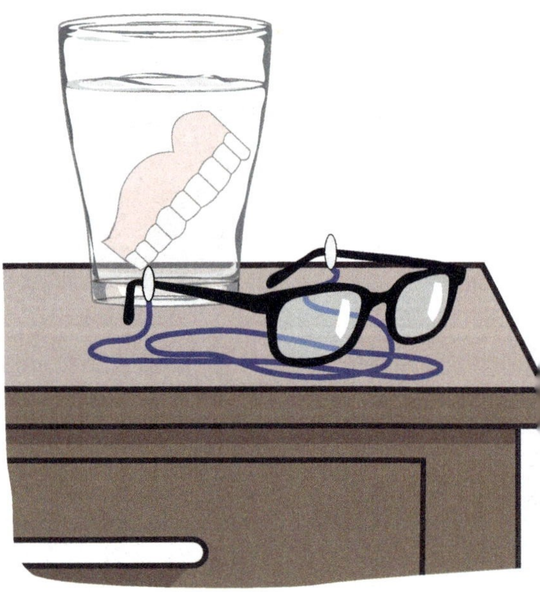

Ensure they **remove their dentures** and that they are cleaned properly and placed in liquid overnight.

Reduce instances of misplaced eyeglasses by putting them in the same visible place. **Get them an eyeglass strap holder** to keep glasses around their neck.

The person with dementia may become attached to a style or outfit and reject other options. If so, consider buying the same outfit, maybe in different colours, but stick to loose-fitting tops, pull-on pants and slip-on shoes.

Bathing

A bath or shower is usually associated with a pleasant part of one's day. That said, helping a loved one to bathe may be a hard thing to do, especially if this person is your spouse, parent or grandparent. It exposes someone in a very intimate way. Be patient and compassionate, and explain that you are there to ensure their safety.

Depending on the stage of dementia, your involvement may only require a helping hand getting everything coordinated. Further along, you may need to assist more or consider getting help from experienced professionals who can safely bathe or shower your loved one.

Always prioritize safety:

- Never leave them alone during bathing once they enter the middle stage of dementia.
- Check the water temperature to avoid injuries.
- Consider a non-skid safety step to add a few inches of height, making getting in and out of the tub easier.
- Switch to a handheld showerhead for more water flow control and to help you wash those hard-to-reach areas.

Tips for a successful bath time:

- Gather all the needed supplies beforehand, such as soap, shampoo, washcloths, towels and moisturizer.
- Ensure the bathroom is relaxing with ambient temperature and soft lighting.
- Encourage them to partake with singing or a story.
- Tell them a treat awaits when they're done, perhaps a sweet snack or a walk. In this way, your loved one will associate bathing with a positive activity.
- Keep to their routine whenever possible. Follow their lead if they prefer bathing in the morning or evening.
- Encourage participation. Let them do as much as possible to feel in control.
- Use non-verbal cues to recognize their need to preserve their dignity. Strategically place towels over their bodies so they feel less exposed.
- If dealing with an older person, scrub softly as their skin is delicate. Pat dry and don't rub the towel in.

If the person with dementia becomes resistant to bathing, preserve their modesty with a robe, close the door and pull the shades down. Use positive encouragement to make them feel capable: *"Using the body wash like that is a great idea. I'm going to do that too."*

Retail websites are a great source for **useful tools** to help make bathing easier. These include dry shampoos, disposable cleansing body wipes, pre-moistened hypoallergenic wash gloves or easy-use bathing capes.

Using the Bathroom and Incontinence

When we were little, our parents told us some topics were not intended for mixed company, like what really goes on in the bathroom. Past generations carried that into adulthood, which is why we still "powder our nose" or "freshen up."

Imagine what it must feel like to lose control of these bodily functions. Incontinence may lead to awkward talks about the need to change undergarments, clothes or bedsheets and result in unscheduled baths or showers.

Tips to navigate bathroom help:

Keep the bathroom door open. Point to it on occasion to see if you get an affirmation reaction.

Keep a clutter-free pathway to the bathroom. There may be a "rush" situation, and this will make it easier to get there.

Schedule regular bathroom trips. Reduced mobility may make it harder to get to the bathroom on time. Help them to the bathroom in the morning and every two hours after that. Include a trip after meals, before outings and right before bed.

Refrain from giving drinks close to bedtime. Avoid beverages that increase urinary output or contain caffeine, including alcohol, coffee, tea or soda.

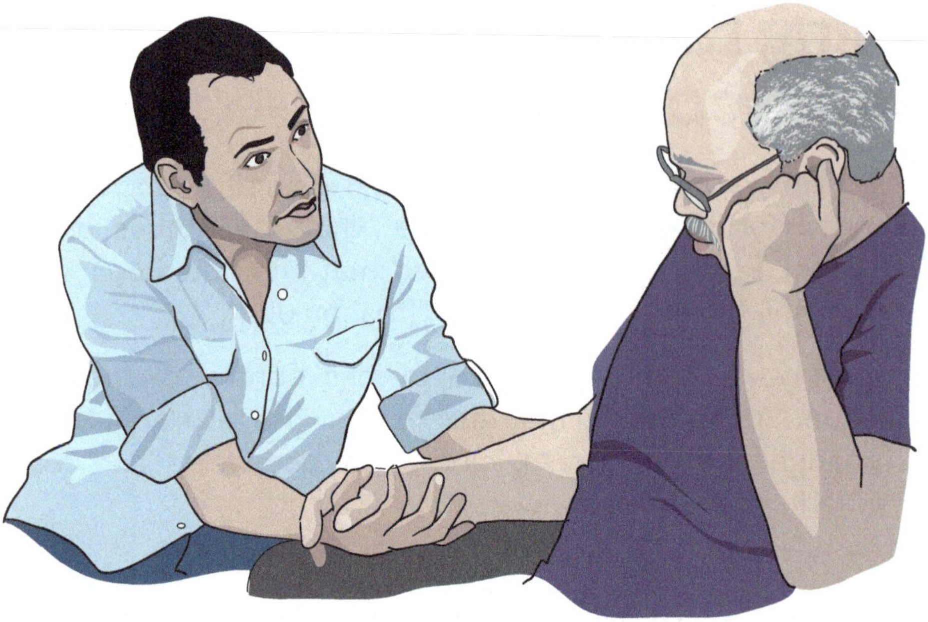

Determine whether they are in any discomfort or pain. Point to their stomachs, left and right sides or back to help localize it.

Set up a doctor's appointment. Tests will rule out weak pelvic muscles, urinary tract infection, enlarged prostate, hemorrhoids or chronic constipation. Medication may be needed. If not, a talk with a doctor can offer other solutions.

Build additional time into your schedule in case incontinence mishaps become part of everyday life.

Look for non-verbal cues. Are they:

- Fidgeting in their chair or pacing back and forth?
- Squeezing their legs together?
- Looking around trying to locate the bathroom?
- Making faces that signal physical distress?

There are many **useful tools** available to help such as absorbent adult briefs, waterproof seat pads, no-rinse peri-wash cleansers, portable bidets, waterproof mattress protectors and skincare barrier creams.

> "The best meals are those prepared by loving hands."
>
> – Ken Poirot

Meals

Think of your kitchen table. Maybe it's a small round bistro style for two or a long rectangle that seats eight. This humble piece of furniture is where you have celebrated milestones, done homework, played games and shared time: lunchtime, dinnertime, teatime. And a person with dementia values those moments just as much as you.

You'll notice that mealtime could become a challenge as dementia progresses. Eating healthy and staying hydrated is important for everyone, especially for a person with dementia. It boosts their energy, and the nutrients help keep other illnesses at bay.

Helpful mealtime tips

Full steam ahead. Do they love to cook? Support your loved one's independence by having them assist with meal preparation: *"How about we prepare your delicious lasagna together?"* Just be around the kitchen to help them out.

Chop, chop. Involve them in the prep work - cutting vegetables, getting out the bowls or breading the chicken. This will also show them that you value their input.

Make it social. Cooking together can deepen your connection, provide time to catch-up and increase the satisfaction of eating the food you prepared together.

Keep it simple. When sharing kitchen duty, only give them one task at a time to avoid feeling overwhelmed or confused.

Sit down and share the meal. This may actually encourage them to eat more. Keep the mood relaxed and don't pressure them to eat at a certain pace.

A healthy, balanced diet includes the following:

Carbohydrates:
starchy vegetables
rice
pasta
honey
fruit juices
and more

Protein:
meat and poultry
fish
eggs
dairy products
beans
legumes
nuts and more

Fibre:
whole grain products
nuts
seeds
beans
fruits and vegetables
and more

As people age, they need fewer calories to maintain their weight. This is due to a slower metabolism and being less physically active. People with dementia tend to eat less, so ensure you prepare their favourites. This may encourage them to eat more. Their favourites may continue to change over time, so check in with them regularly.

Watch for non-verbal cues:

- Does a frown mean the food is too hot or too spicy?
- Does "blah" mean they don't like the taste?
- Does running their tongue across their teeth mean a piece of food is stuck?
- Does a smile mean they are enjoying it and that you should make that again?
- Does moving the plate away mean they don't like it, are full or would rather eat later?
- Does tracking the plate with their eyes from the counter to table indicate they are hungry or anxious?
- Does pointing to an item mean they want more?

Communicate with your own cues:

- Ask *"Do you like/don't like that?"* while pointing at each individual item on the plate.
- Taste the food yourself to test for heat, spiciness, acidity or sweetness levels.
- Tell them what they're eating. Point to it and make pleasant sounds like *"Yum."*

Helpful recommendations:

- Avoid too much salt or sugar. Keep the sugar bowl and saltshaker out of sight.
- Use herbs and seasoning to add flavour to dishes.
- Use white plates to highlight colours and textures.
- If their appetite decreases, try planning smaller meals more frequently.
- If a reduced appetite leads to weight loss, consider adding nutritional supplements to daily meals.
- Keep track of when and where they prefer to eat. Maybe they always had lunch at 11 a.m. on a TV tray and dinner at the kitchen table. Seat them in their usual place. This will encourage them to eat more.
- Include finger foods and set aside utensils. This may persuade them to eat more frequently.
- If they don't finish their meals, offer nutritious snacks to eat during the day. Leave them out and clearly visible. Point to them on occasion.

- Cut foods items into manageable bite-size pieces. A pizza is a pizza, anyway you slice it.
- Don't react negatively to spilled food or liquids. It is what it is. Just be pleased they're eating.
- Prepare make-ahead meals to save time and effort.
- Encourage them to drink water during the meal, indeed all through the day. Use their favourite cup. Soups, juices and teas are also considered sources of fluid.
- Should swallowing become an issue, opt for softer foods or use a blender or food processor.
- Create an environment they like - be it background sounds or complete silence.
- Regularly check the fridge for spoiled or expired food.

Step-by-step activity planning

Keeping up interests and pastimes helps everyone stay more active, sleep better and maintain a positive attitude. With dementia, all that is needed is a little creative planning on your part. And what matters is to focus on the things they can do and not what they cannot do.

Practical tips to get them moving

Establish what time of day their energy level is highest and try to do the activity at that time of the day.

Be prepared. Let's think gardening. Get all the tools ready as visual clues. Gather up gloves, rake, hose and shovels in one place and say, *"These hydrangeas are going to look beautiful in that corner."*

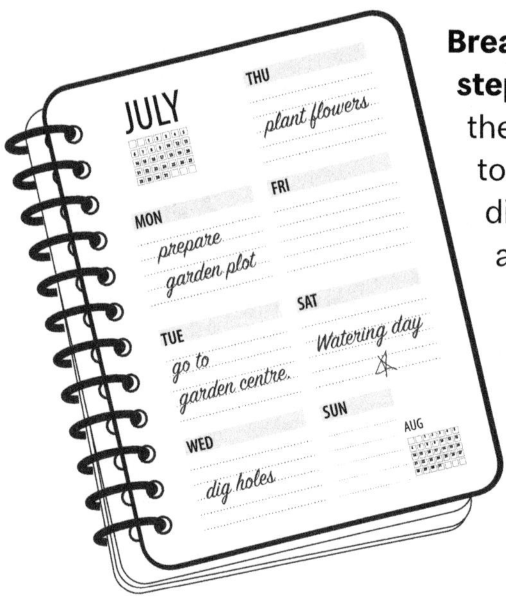

Break up tasks into manageable daily steps. Each day you can do one of these things: Go to the garden centre to select flowers, turn over the soil, dig the holes, plant the flowers and add the mulch.

Schedule weekly steps: These could include grooming, trimming or watering the plants, lawn or hedges. This will help hold their interest.

Learn to adjust. There's always a way. When it becomes more demanding, look into gardening stools or knee pads to help them. This will promote a sense of ownership and purpose.

Bike it if they love to cycle. Signal the outing by pointing to the helmets or jackets. When balance becomes an issue, consider bike stabilizer wheels or three-wheel adult bikes.

Be the cool care partner. Download computer or phone games for regular recreation and enjoyment.

As flexibility and strength diminish, explore exercises that can be done from a chair, bed or a pool. Do the moves together or help by moving their arms and legs in various positions. This will ensure muscles are engaged and stimulated.

Revisit their favourite places

Doing something memorable gives a person with dementia - in fact all of us - a purpose. Ask what they would like to do; there may be something they miss that would make them happy.

Sit on the park bench under the tree with just the right amount of shade: *"So this is where you escaped to Saturday mornings."*

Go to the coffee shop with the perfect blueberry scones: *"Everyone seems to know you here."*

Visit their place of worship for comfort and a sense of peace. It may also be an opportunity to socialize with old friends.

Go for a drive along a familiar stretch of road. Tell them you can see why they always liked the area.

Be open to their ideas and be spontaneous. Be enthusiastic if they suggest something new.

Bring on the classics. Music can evoke many fond memories and creates a fun and relaxing atmosphere to be enjoyed by everyone.

No matter what they do, praise them for succeeding and for trying when they stumble or fall short.

> "My hope for the future is for more care, compassion and understanding. People with dementia did not choose this path. Those of us living with it take one day at a time, enjoying the good days left and keeping our special memories."
>
> – Carol-Ann, care partner to her husband Stan, Alzheimer's Society of Canada

Challenging Behaviour

Dementia is much like the four seasons. With shifting weather conditions, you adapt. You switch from coats to t-shirts, and thoughts of an afternoon spent reading wrapped up in a warm blanket turn to eagerness for a stroll in the garden.

When caring for a person with dementia, **you also must adapt to shifts in their symptoms.** There are two points of view at play - yours and that of the person with dementia. They may not see or interpret the situation, or your efforts, in the same way. From their point of view, **you are the one who doesn't get it.**

You know how you can tell immediately when someone close to you is upset. It's not hard because you know them so well. When it comes to a person with dementia, you must put in that extra time, because it can be hard. You'll need to pay attention, stay calm and pinpoint triggers.

A step-by-step investigative approach. By applying the process of elimination, you can zero in on what they are trying to communicate. Ask questions, consider the whole situation and use non-verbal cues.

Is it physical?

Do they seem agitated at mealtime and do they eat enough?

- Did you start a new meal service, and the food is upsetting their stomach? Does it constipate them?
- Have they become lactose-intolerant? Do they become anxious when milk or cheese are served?
- Have they acquired a new dislike for certain foods?
- Do they resent the fact that no one asked them what they wanted to eat?

Do they seem to be more fidgety or nervous?

- Did you buy a new detergent that irritates their skin or has a scent they don't like?
- Do they dislike the colour of the shirt they are wearing and want to take it off?

Do they no longer want to take daily walks?

- Did you change their footwear? Are the shoes too tight and they now have painful blisters?
- Is there a new dog in the area that barks loudly at them when they walk by?

Afternoons were when they were most energetic. Now all they want to do is nap.

Did they:

- Start a new medication?
- Alter their eating habits or reduce their caffeine?

Is it emotional?

Do they seem withdrawn and reserved?

- Did they forget that the neighbour they waved to every morning has moved away? Is this why they keep pointing at the window?
- Is their usual part-time care partner away? Do they seem listless when their replacement is in the house?
- Do they ignore you when you tell them what to do? Could they resent your authoritative tone?
- Did they fail to recognize someone and it made them sad?

Do they seem more anxious or suspicious?

- Did they forget you stored away items in the closet or garage? Do they think someone broke in?
- Have you moved the furniture around and they don't like the new layout?
- Did you remove the family photo to have the frame repaired? Could they be missing a cherished memory?

- Have you installed new locks on the door, or an alarm system, and they feel trapped and panicky?
- Did you change their routine because of your work schedule? Could they be struggling to adjust?
- Do they start to tap their hands constantly? Have they been sitting all afternoon watching TV? Could they be bored or have unspent energy?
- Do they pace around the room? Is someone new coming over? Was their trip to the market postponed? Is there a thunderstorm outside?

Is it their environment?

Did they start to yell, curse or even lash out physically?

- Has the school nearby upgraded their sound system and the loud bell agitates them? Is it the same reaction when an ambulance rushes down the street? Could it be sensory overload?
- Did you tell them that they are late for an appointment, so they'll have to bathe, get dressed and eat before leaving. Could listing the multiple tasks have overwhelmed them?
- Do the bright headlights and engine roar from the adjoining driveway wake them up at night?
- Did you argue with your spouse or discipline your child in front of them? Are they feeling scared or protective of their grandchild?

Just like anyone, **a person living with dementia reacts to what is around them**. This is their perception of reality. It is an exercise in futility to try and convince them otherwise. That will only serve to intensify a delicate situation.

What it should do is give you the incentive to take a step back and see things from their perspective. In doing so, you will be better positioned to meet their needs.

- If something in their environment upsets them, show them that you are removing it.
- Reduce distractions. Turn off the TV, computer screen, whirling overhead fan, and mute your phone.
- Redirect their attention to a different activity. Lead them into another room, engage them with a puzzle or game, go outside for a walk or read to them.

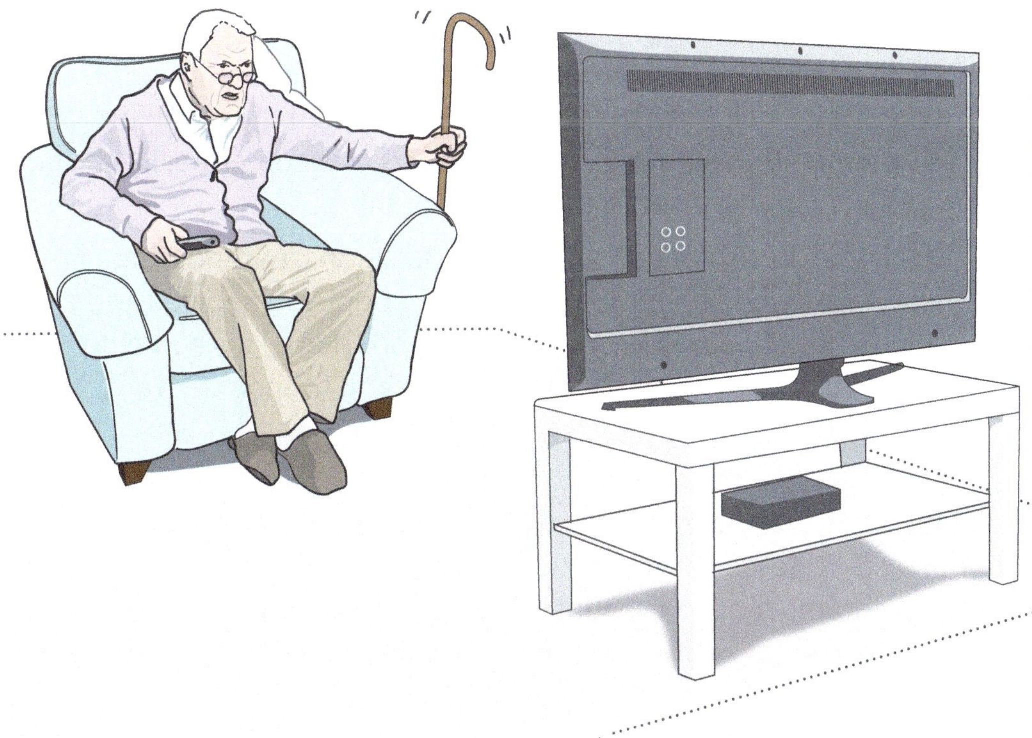

Hallucinations, delusions and paranoia

These three symptoms can be especially difficult to manage and are a jolting reminder of the profound effect dementia has on thinking and behaviour. These displays of distorted reality truly reveal how cognitive impairment changes the brain. The flare-ups can be highly emotional, and learning ways to restore calm and composure are crucial.

- **Hallucinations:** This involves seeing, hearing, smelling or tasting something that doesn't exist and that no one else experiences. To a person living with dementia, though, it is very real. There are two facets to these symptoms. Some hallucinations may feel threatening, such as someone creeping around the shadows or hearing an echoing whisper, while others may be quite pleasant, like seeing a beloved pet or smelling something baking in the oven.
- **Delusions:** These are false beliefs that contradict facts or truth. Once someone with dementia is convinced of something, it can be incredibly difficult to dissuade them of their opinion. A common delusion is being convinced that someone, like a nurse or care partner, is stealing from them.
- **Paranoia:** In a direct offshoot from delusions, paranoia sets in when a person living with dementia become suspicious and distrustful of people or activities around them. This could be directed at care partners, close family and friends or even strangers.

Provide both verbal reassurance and physical comfort to show empathy. Distract their attention. It is especially important with these three symptoms that you validate their fears and refrain from arguing with them. You will defuse the situation much faster by dodging a confrontation.

Consult with their doctor to assess the new symptoms and to rule out any other medical causes such as vision problems, infections, migraines or a side effect of medication.

Be vigilant of what they are viewing on TV. Don't leave it running continuously on one channel without checking the program line-up. Shows with heightening drama or suspense could trigger delusions or paranoia.

Adjust the physical environment. Dim or increase the lights, draw the curtains, remove mirrors, cover glass-top tables and blow out the candles to reduce shadows, glare, flickering glows or misleading silhouettes.

Consider duplicates of the items they frequently misplace, such as eyeglasses, hairbrush, coffee mug or slippers.

> "No matter how many mistakes you make or how slow you progress, you are still way ahead of everyone who isn't trying."
>
> – Tony Robbins

Care Partner Self-Care

Make a deliberate choice today, this very minute. Choose to prioritize self-care. A mindful approach to your own well-being now will have long-range benefits, especially as you move forward through this dementia journey. Time and emotions are precious commodities. When "care partner" becomes another title in your inventory of life roles, self-care is often neglected. Many things may be out of your control but looking out for your own physical and emotional health need not be one of them. The only way to successfully go the distance as a care partner is to **take care of yourself**.

Have that internal dialogue

Acknowledge your thoughts and emotions. You are entitled to each and every one of them. **It's OK.**

Accept yourself for who you are, including your strengths and weaknesses. **It's OK.**

Forgive yourself. Choose emotional freedom. Don't waste time on negative self-judgement. **It's OK.**

Know you will make mistakes. Leave room for them. They do not characterize all of you as a care partner. **It's OK.**

Learn about dementia now and learn more as you go. Define and redefine your own expectations and goals instead of trying to fulfill those of other people. **It's OK.**

Like the person living with dementia, realize you too will have good days and bad days. **It's OK.**

Accept that you may love the person you are caring for, but there may be moments when you don't like them. **It's OK.**

Acknowledge that you may feel lonely and grieve for them when they no longer interact with you as they used to. **It's OK.**

Self-care is not selfish. It will make you stronger so that you have the energy to care for someone else. **It's OK.**

Don't set yourself up to be a hero. You're not a rescuer, you're a care partner. Just be there. **It's OK.**

Start with a healthy foundation

In Section 1, we talked about how vital **SEE** was to a person with dementia. It also pertains to you as a care partner.

Sleep well

Eat properly

Exercise regularly

Though it may be hard some days, getting a healthy supply of these three basics will promote your resilience and strength, making you a better partner.

No doubt, you consistently aim to treat the person you care for with affection and kindness. Look in the mirror and do the same for that person as well.

Seek solutions

Talk to your own health care professional and get a complete checkup. Tell them about how you're eating, sleeping, managing stress, what kind of help you are receiving and how you are feeling.

Follow through on their recommendation to see a therapist, if this is a feasible option. Find one you feel comfortable with, as you will be discussing uncomfortable topics. Consider what factors you deem essential - location, gender or age. Do you want someone who is faith-based? Do you want a general therapist, someone with a specialty in family dynamics or expertise in care partner issues?

Talk to your spouse, friends, and family members about the reality of providing support to a person with dementia. In speaking candidly about it, they will be better positioned to understand the scope of your commitment as well as your occasional bouts of irritability or tiredness.

Look into a care partner support group. There you will encounter people who face similar day-to-day struggles. Your shared experiences in a safe space allow for an open exchange of feelings and coping strategies. It may also help lessen your sense of isolation or loneliness.

Ask for help. This can be difficult to do. It doesn't mean you're not capable. It just means sometimes IT'S HARD. No one benefits if you are exhausted or irritable. You may also be surprised how much people want to help. Again, if possible, hire professionals to manage some day-to-day activities.

Provide concrete examples. Now that you have their attention, move beyond the vague "I need help." Be prepared with a list - errands, groceries, laundry, etc. Secondary or informal partners may be more at ease with assigned tasks. You can all figure out how to tag-team priorities together.

"Be strong enough to face the world each day.

Be weak enough to know you cannot do everything alone."

– Author Unknown

Investigate local resources

Community centres have a variety of adult day programs. Some may even have adapted exercise classes, such as aqua fitness, tai chi, or stretching. This can give the person with dementia an opportunity to exercise or socialize while you get a needed respite or "me time."

Call colleges or universities and look into hiring a student. There could be internship programs in place. Choose someone studying medicine, nursing, physiotherapy, kinesiology, rehabilitation or geriatrics for some hands-on experience. This exchange could be free of charge or less expensive than professional assistance.

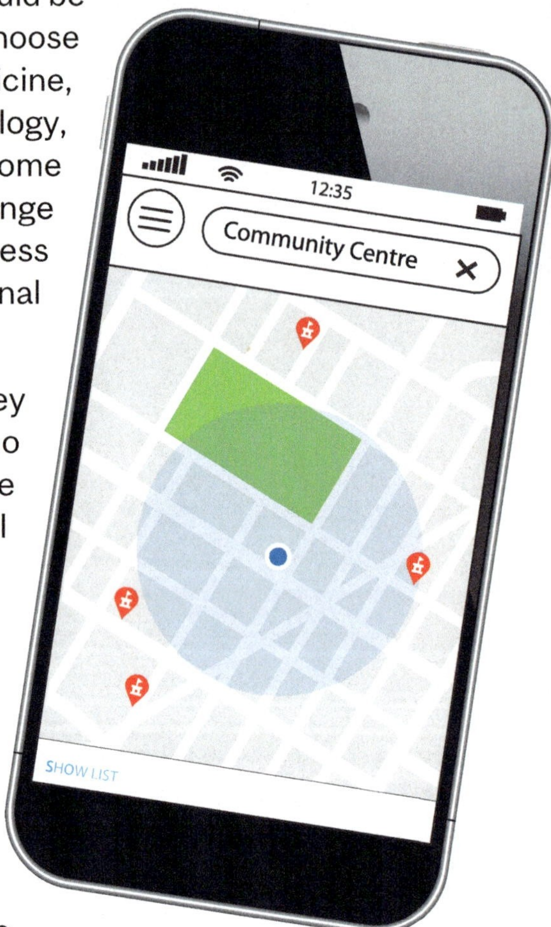

Call retirement residences. They may have a list of people who volunteer or who work part-time and may want some additional hours.

Inquire at local universities or the Alzheimer's Society about dementia research studies. You could enroll your person if they meet the qualifications. Not only would this provide the medical community with valuable insight, but it could also be a social outlet for them and a break for you.

Do yourself a favour

Let go of the mindset that no one else can do it as well as you. It may be true, but don't let it stop you from getting help.

Be more flexible. If you didn't get to everything you'd hoped to accomplish in a given day, make your peace with that. The floor isn't mopped, the dishwasher isn't loaded - how significant is that in the end? Take the pressure off yourself.

Join your local gym and sign up for a class. Got kids? Find a gym that also provides babysitting services. You'll feel energized and refreshed and your kids will have fun.

Meet up with a friend. No time or funds to devote to a class? Get together for 30 minutes whenever possible to release those endorphins. Go to a nearby park or each other's homes.

Multitask. Is your workplace nearby? Opt to walk to work. You'll exercise, enjoy the fresh air and clear your head.

Put the car keys away. Consider taking public transportation and avoid the frustration of rush hour traffic. Instead, meditate, listen to a book, daydream or enjoy the entertainment value of people-watching.

Street smart. If neither of these options are viable, then hit the road while listening to a thought-provoking podcast or a stand-up routine to start your day with knowledge or humour.

A network of one

There may be a few reasons you find yourself coping alone as a care partner to someone living with dementia:

- You are an only child with no extended family.
- You've recently moved into the area and have yet to make new connections.
- You're an introvert who doesn't easily make friends.

Make that connection

Get informed. Speak to their health care professional or support staff of nurses and coordinators. They could share various resources to guide you in the right direction for help.

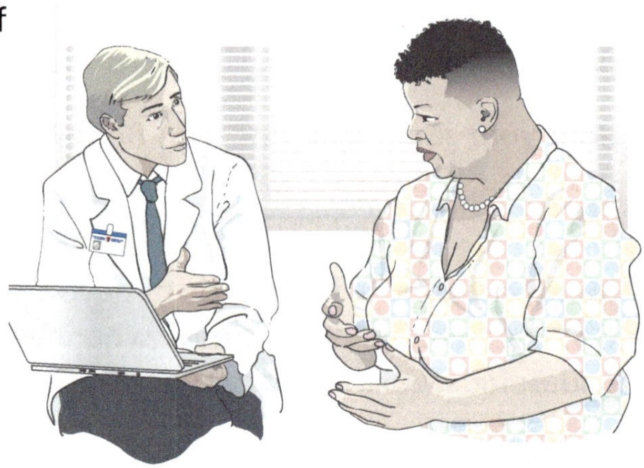

Get support. Look for care partner online forums or chat rooms. The anonymity to speak freely while also getting the information and inspiration you seek could be your answer.

Get connected. Join an online support group. You may be more comfortable with that than with face-to-face interaction.

Get advice. Call a care partner helpline. The operators are well versed in the issues you confront on a daily basis.

Get networking. Speak to your human resources representative at work. There may be programs in place to assist care partners.

Get friendly. A batch of goodies can sweeten the deal when meeting the neighbours. In return, they may have valuable information about your family member, provide their contact information or offer to help with tasks like lawn care, moving the recycling bins or shovelling the snow.

Young care partners

We all have certain expectations at different stages of our lives, especially when younger. Some imagine and plan for a happy and successful future while others direct their energy to fully living in the present.

Whatever is your preferred "living the good life" vibe, very few people anticipate becoming care partners at a young age. It can be a very jarring way to enter adulthood.

Find someone to confide in, preferably outside your family circle. You'll be able to speak openly and get some objective advice. This could be a counsellor, teacher or coach.

Speak to your family members as well. Tell them what is going on at home so they can provide appropriate guidance.

Find your safe place. Is it in your best friend's basement to play video games? Is it the corner deli or the library steps with a handful of pencils and an open sketchbook? Make a point of going there often to recharge your batteries.

Plan ahead. An outing to a concert or amusement park will give you something to look forward to and break up your routine. Happy anticipation is a good thing.

Seek out people who lift you up - praise and motivation are critical to someone who is still growing and learning. Avoid those who are negative and critical of your situation, or who try to help you cope by encouraging reckless behaviour. Make changes to your circle of friends if needed.

As with adult care partners, you are urged to ask for help. It may be more readily available to you than you think. And, this could remind you to be young and young at heart.

Care partner burnout

There is nothing like being a care partner to make you feel like you are "burning the candle at both ends." And if you are constantly angry or bitter, you may just "burn your bridges."

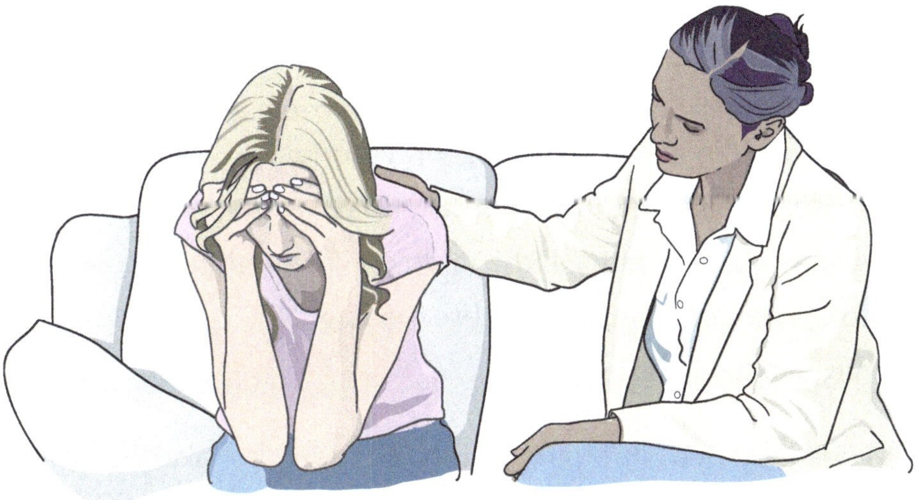

In other words, care partner burnout is something you want to watch out for and avoid. Supporting someone with dementia is demanding and as the condition progresses, can be all-consuming. You may have to give up quite a bit in your life. Reduced work hours may prevent you from getting a promotion, frequent doctor's appointments may mean you miss out on your kids' science fairs, ball games or graduations and feeling drained may affect your inclination to enjoy intimacy with your partner.

On the other hand, if you're past retirement age, the physical demands needed may become too strenuous, your dream travel plans may be derailed, or you may find that your social activities are often cancelled and you suddenly find yourself spending more time alone.

It can also affect your perception of how vital it is to maintain the **SEE** principle mentioned earlier - your ability to sleep well, eat properly and exercise regularly.

Recognize the signs of care partner burnout in yourself:

- Angry outbursts directed at the person living with dementia or other individuals in your life;
- Crying over minor upsets;
- Feelings of sadness, emptiness or hopelessness;
- Withdrawal from activities or hobbies you used to enjoy or disinterest in social gathering with friends;
- Decreased energy, both mental and physical;
- Waking up frequently in the middle of the night;
- Noticeable changes in appetite or weight;
- Inexplicable illnesses.

Strategies outlined throughout this section are also relevant to avoiding burnout. Ask others for help, open up to someone close to you, a health care professional or support group, stay in touch with friends and indulge in some "me time."

Avoid harmful lifestyle choices

All care partners seek respite from their overwhelming responsibilities. However, say no to these shortcuts:

- Excessive alcohol or drug consumption;
- Overuse of prescription medication;
- Unhealthy eating habits (overeating or undereating);
- No physical activity;
- Self-imposed isolation and avoiding other people;
- Discontinuing activities that brought you joy.

Look for ways to reward yourself:

- Gather pictures and clippings of your cherished memories and start a scrapbook or photo album.
- Make homemade gifts like jams, candles or jewellery.
- Spend time in your workshop making furniture or assorted crafts.
- Get a group together to play pool, bingo or cards.
- Arrange playdates. Rotating childcare twice a month guarantees you some alone time.
- Say "No" to people who don't add positive energy to your life. The more boundaries you set, the easier it will become to hold firm.
- Take a look at your calendar and find that 30 minutes a day for yourself. Do something you like... or do nothing. Both are good.
- Chat with a friend who lifts your spirits, go see a comedy or watch beloved old TV shows.
- Do things to feed your inner spirit and rejuvenate yourself. Spend a few minutes meditating, writing in a journal, doing mindful breathing exercises or stretching.
- Go for a run, walk, bike ride, drive. Just go.

Finally, though it may sometimes be difficult, find the positive in any given day. Dementia does not spell the end of happy times together. Focus on your relationship and remember that while you may be their care partner, you were first a cherished and valued person in their life. Whether that be their spouse, partner, child, grandchild, sibling or friend, the foundation of your relationship started there. And that's where you continue to build.

Summary

The goal of an effective care partner is to develop a shared language and understanding, and to forge a solid relationship between you and the person living with dementia.

Care partners are partners in care. They actively participate and support a person with dementia in their tasks of daily living.

There are four types of care partners - primary, secondary, informal and professional.

Stages of emotions for care partners include denial, empathy, frustration, fear and guilt.

Understanding verbal and non-verbal cues, as well as adapting your own, is critical to being an effective care partner and communicator.

Navigating family dynamics may give rise to disputes and tension. Implement practical solutions to minimize conflict.

Establish routines for grooming, bathing, dressing, using the bathroom, meals and activities to improve a person with dementia's quality of life and promote their self-confidence.

Determine whether challenging behaviours are provoked by physical, emotional or environmental causes.

Self-care is vital for your well-being and for preventing care partner burnout. Ask for help and look for viable solutions.

Resources

Most countries have local, provincial, state or national initiatives, programs and resources available to you. Search the internet for help, support and services in your area for people living with dementia and their care partners.

McGill University Health Centre (MUHC)

Division of Geriatric Medicine
MUHC Montreal General Hospital
Tel.: 514-934-1934, ext. 34499
Website: www.mcgill.ca/geriatrics

Division of Geriatric Medicine
Jewish General Hospital
Tel.: 514-340-7501
Fax: 514-340-7547

McGill Dementia Education Program (DEP)

McGill University Faculty of Medicine and Health Sciences
Website: www.mcgill.ca/dementia
www.mcgill.ca/geriatrics/dementia-education-program
Email: dementia@mcgill.ca

Alzheimer's Disease International

Website: www.alzint.org
Email: info@alzint.org

Alzheimer Society of Canada

Tel.: 416-488-8772
Toll-free: 1-800-616-8816
Fax: 416-322-6656

Website: www.alzheimer.ca
Email: info@alzheimer.ca

Federation of Quebec Alzheimer Societies

Fax: 514-369-7900
Website: alzheimer.ca/federationquebecoise/en
Email: info@alzheimerquebec.ca

Alzheimer Society of Montreal

Tel.: 514-369-0800
Fax: 514-369-4103
Website: alzheimermontreal.ca/en/
Email: info@alzheimermontreal.ca

Caregiver Support – L'Appui

Tel.: 514-789-2460
Toll-free: 1-855-852-7784
Fax: 514-787-1995
Website: www.lappui.org/en
Email: info-aidant@lappui.org

Grace Dart Foundation

Tel.: 514-742-9853
Website: fondationgracedart.com
Email: info@fondationgracedart.org

NOTES